BRUCE A. RAY

CELEBRATING

THE

SABBATH

finding rest in
a restless world

PUBLISHING

P.O.BOX 817 • PHILLIPSBURG • NEW JERSEY 08865-0817

Unless otherwise indicated, all Scripture quotations are from the HOLY BIBLE, NEW INTERNATIONAL VERSION®. NIV®. Copyright © 1973, 1978, 1984 by International Bible Society. Used by permission of Zondervan Publishing House. All rights reserved. Italics indicate emphasis added.

Page Design by Tobias Design
Typesetting by Michelle Feaster

Printed in the United States of America

Library of Congress Cataloging-in-Publication Data

Ray, Bruce A., 1947-
    Celebrating the sabbath : finding rest in a restless world /
Bruce A. Ray.
      p. cm.
    Includes bibliographical references.
    ISBN 0-87552-394-3 (alk. paper)
    1. Sunday—Biblical teaching. 2. Sabbath—Biblical teaching.
3. Christian life. I. Title.
BS680.S17 R39 2000
263'.1—dc21   99-058578

CELEBRATING
THE
SABBATH

This book is
lovingly dedicated
to the members and alumni of
Juanita Community Church,
with whom I have enjoyed
more than a thousand Sabbaths
to the glory of God.

CONTENTS

FOREWORD

Revival never produces permanent health in God's people. It suddenly resuscitates them, but daily good habits of worship and sanctification must conserve and nourish the spiritual health given from above. Each of the great judges (in the biblical book named for their office) led weakened saints nearer to God. The effects of these rapid, corporate surges forward endured only twenty or eighty years. Then the decay of religious life became sadly obvious again. Yet the deterioration began soon after the advance and proceeded gradually until major defections appeared.

For those who have experienced any degree of revival, it is transformed too soon into a memory, a matter of nostalgia. Perhaps it is only as churches decline bit by bit that their members realize that in former days they were privileged to live through a special Spirit-given infusion of fresh life.

This book recognizes that we must, in Jesus' words, "Wake up! Strengthen what remains and is about to die" (Revelation 3:2). We have a responsibility to cherish God's spiritual blessings. One of the great divinely appointed means of preserving and nourishing the received showers of God's grace is the Sabbath institution. Properly observed, the Sabbath can both renew animation of our hearts in the love of God and slow the decline in our appreciation of what God has given us.

A tidal wave of anti-Sabbath influences is crashing against the modern church. There have been local, denominational, and national advances in life, truth, and righteousness during this century that can only be attributed to the Spirit of God. However, they are in imminent danger of being utterly overwhelmed and reversed as the Sabbath and thus worship are neglected.

Pastor Bruce Ray has made a major effort to shore up our understanding and practice of Sabbath keeping. *Celebrating the Sabbath* is delightful reading about a recurring day of delight. How we need these principles and wise directions related to the fourth commandment! Beneath the text of this book may be felt the rhythm of constant pastoral concern for the well-being of Christ's church. May God use this work to keep our churches from being swamped by secular ideas and old paths of disobedience that provoke God's displeasure.

—WALTER J. CHANTRY

ACKNOWLEDGMENTS

Special thanks are due to my family and to the members, deacons, and elders of Juanita Community Church who encouraged me to put this material into written form and then gave me the time to do it (no more excuses!). Elisha Riedlinger used the gifts that the Spirit gave him and gleaned parts from other antique computers to keep my old PC running. Ray Berett, Furb Jolley, Steve Kringle, and Kerry Smith all served as readers and furnished me with innumerable and invaluable suggestions throughout the project. Steve Harris moved here from Idaho to help with pastoral responsibilities so I could write. Finally, I want to thank my wife and partner in every work I do. It's not easy being married to someone who gets his best ideas after he has gone to bed and then has to get up to write them down. Terri, I love you!

ONE

MCSABBATH

The Son of Man is Lord
even of the Sabbath.
—*Mark 2:28*

O day of rest and gladness,
O day of joy and light,
O balm of care and sadness,
Most beautiful, most bright;
On thee the high and lowly,
Through ages joined in tune,
Sing Holy, Holy, Holy,
To the great God Triune.
—*Christopher Wordsworth, 1862*

AN AMERICAN ICON

"Did somebody say *McDonald's?*"

That familiar line from radio and television advertising works well because almost everyone recognizes the McDonald's name and associates it with fast-food restaurants.

Like baseball, apple pie, and Chevrolet, McDonald's is an American icon. With missionary zeal, McDonald's has spread success among its franchisees throughout much of the world. Indeed, some even see McDonald's as a taming and civilizing agent in the world, and the Golden Arches as the new symbol of world peace. I am not sure if it is true, but a friend insists that no two countries having McDonald's restaurants have ever gone to war with each other!

As an icon, McDonald's presents an image, or a picture, of some of the best and some of the worst of Western civilization at the dawn of the twenty-first century. To its credit, McDonald's shows us how corporate America can deliver its products to consumers with consistent quality, efficiency, and economy. Wherever you go in the world, you can expect to find an acceptable hamburger, a clean restaurant, friendly service, and affordable prices under the Golden Arches. To our embarrassment, the reason *why* McDonald's is so tremendously successful is that the rest of us are living life at such a frenzied pace that sometimes a Big Mac with fries and a Diet Coke is the best we can do for dinner. We don't have time for anything else. Indeed, that's our excuse for a lot of things: *we just don't have enough time.* We, like others in our society, are too busy working hard to earn money so we can "shop 'til we drop."

McDonald's is not to blame for our lives of perpetual

motion, but the corporate giant clearly profits from our busyness. That's why in Israel McDonald's has become an icon of a different kind. The owner of the Ramat Aviv shopping mall in Tel Aviv wants all the stores in his mall to conform to Jewish dietary laws and to close on the Jewish Sabbath. There's nothing unusual about that. But for the McDonald's in the mall, this means no cheeseburgers (dairy products and meat may not be mixed), and it means closing from sundown on Friday to sundown on Saturday.

Omri Padan, the owner of thirty-seven McDonald's outlets in Israel, thinks that will be bad for profits. He plans to defy the mall owner and take the dispute to court. "I see this as part of our war to run like a free business in a Western country, like in Europe and the U.S.," Padan declares.[1]

Profits and piety are colliding in Tel Aviv, and the Golden Arches are really and symbolically caught in the cross fire. Note the terminology of the combatants. Padan maintains that as a businessman he is "at war" and identifies his enemy as the Sabbath (and, by implication, its Giver). Traditional piety must yield to profitability, for no one can serve "both God and Money" (Matthew 6:24), and it seems that Money has more loyal and committed subjects in the world today than God does. *Seattle Times* staff columnist Erik Lacitis, in a tongue-in-cheek commentary advocating an updated Ten Commandments, offers this version of the fourth one:

> Remember the Sabbath day, to keep it holy. Unless you're the head of a national discount chain. What, and lose all that Sunday business?[2]

SABBATH CONFLICT

Conflict over the Sabbath is nothing new. Disagreements about the Sabbath have raged in and out of the church for many centuries. Those seeking profit and pleasure have often been impatient with the Lord's command to rest, and have chafed under it. People who think the world exists for their own personal peace and affluence have never embraced God's command to abstain from work and to rest as he did. The prophet Amos exposed the greed and dishonest business practices of merchants in his day, who only tolerated the Sabbath, but never enjoyed it. They complained within themselves,

> "When will the New Moon be over that we may sell grain, and the Sabbath be ended that we may market wheat?"—skimping the measure, boosting the price and cheating with dishonest scales, buying the poor with silver and the needy for a pair of sandals, selling even the sweepings with the wheat. (Amos 8:5–6)

Many people see the Sabbath, or Lord's Day, as an infringement of their personal liberty—a day that God has *taken from* them instead of a gift that he has *given to* them for rest, worship, and celebration. The modern world, they argue, is too complex to set apart a whole day for rest and worship. There is too much that we *need* to do and too much that we *want* to do to give up one day in seven for God. We are just too busy.

As some unknown observer has described modern America, "We worship our work, we work at our play, and we play at our worship." People simply do not take Sunday seriously anymore as a day dedicated to holy uses.

Some churches are responding by offering abbreviated worship services on other days of the week. One man told me that his church was adding brief, informal, Saturday night worship services to their schedule. The reason for the additional meeting is that they are located in an area that offers many recreational opportunities that compete with traditional Sunday morning services. By having church services on Saturday night, people can have the whole day on Sunday to go hiking, sailing, shopping, or whatever else they want to do, without being inconvenienced by having to attend services. We can just fit God into our schedules the way we do piano lessons and dental appointments. Then, if something more interesting comes along, we can always reschedule! Some churches have changed to Friday night services, and one congregation in our area has services only on Thursday nights, so that those craving even more recreation can have the whole weekend for their enjoyment without any spiritual interruption.

McSabbath is here—worship services that are quick, easy, convenient, and user-friendly. No muss, no fuss. Little or no sacrifice required. Consumers can be in and out in under an hour. McSermons may not be as nutritional as the real thing, but, like Big Macs, they have a predictable quality that fills a void at least for a while. The question is, however, do they fulfill the *purpose* of worship, which is to *please God?*

Conflicts occur when what we want to do on the Sabbath clashes with what pleases God, when our will contradicts his.[3] Am *I* the Lord of the Sabbath and therefore free to do whatever I please, or is the Son of Man? Is it *my* day or *his?*

SABBATH DELIGHT

Long ago, Isaiah told us that the way to find delight in the Sabbath and to experience joy in the Lord is to subordinate our pleasures to his, to make God's will our own (Isaiah 58:13–14). The goal of the redeemed heart is always to please the Redeemer.[4] As Walter Chantry notes,

> A heart that loves the Lord will leap for joy at the prospect of a day with him. Doesn't a child love to have a day with his father? Of course the worldly will loathe giving any time to God. The self-absorbed will regret any day spent in his presence. Without love for God such a requirement will seem narrow and a heavy burden. But for the godly it is a broad road of liberty and joy. There is an entire day each week liberated from my ordinary recreations and labours to serve the lover of my soul and to be with him.[5]

Isn't that what we ask whenever we pray in the Lord's Prayer, "Your kingdom come, your will be done on earth as it is in heaven" (Matthew 6:10)?

Well, this introductory chapter has to end sometime. I'd like to linger here a little longer, but I really don't have time. I have far too much to do, and the week is already half over. I am busy writing a book, but I also have to take the car in for repairs, pick up my daughter after school, and stop at the library—and tonight is the choir association meeting!

In the pages that follow, we will survey biblical teaching

concerning the Sabbath and the Lord's Day. If you are looking for the final, definitive, answer-every-question book on
the Sabbath that will overcome every objection and con-
vince every doubter, this isn't it. I am not writing primarily
to the scholars in the crowd. They tend to write to each
other, and the work they do is necessary, even if it doesn't always seem practical. But I am writing primarily to those of
you who work hard five or six days a week and would like to
know how God wants you to enjoy the seventh.

My goal is to be biblical, practical, and brief. I think I'll
refill my coffee, though, before we continue. Would you like
another cup—to go?

REVIEW

1. What is an icon? Do you agree with the observation that
   McDonald's is "an American icon" representing some
   of the best and some of the worst of Western civilization? Why or why not?
2. What is a common excuse we often use for not doing
   what we know we should be doing?
3. How valid is this excuse? Why are *you* so busy? How important are the things that keep you busy?
4. How has McDonald's in Israel become a symbol of the
   Sabbath wars?
5. What two motives do many people have for opposing a
   day set apart for rest, worship, and celebration?
6. How are many churches responding to current social
   attitudes concerning the Sabbath? How is your church
   responding?

7. What are Sabbath wars? Have you ever experienced such conflicts within yourself?

8. What is the goal of every redeemed heart? How does this help us to find delight in the Sabbath?

RESPONSE

1. Is my life a life of perpetual motion? Do I have times when I can be quiet and still, or am I busy every moment of every day?

2. What are my own attitudes toward the Sabbath? Do I welcome or resent this day of rest?

3. Do I prefer McSabbath over the real thing? Do I get uptight when the sermon or prayers have gone longer than I think they should?

4. What Sabbath conflicts do I have in my own heart and life right now? What is God calling me to do that I don't want to do? What do I want to do that God may not want me to do?

5. Is it really my goal to please God in everything I do (2 Corinthians 5:9)?

TWO

THE FOURTH COMMANDMENT

Remember the Sabbath day
by keeping it holy.
—*Exodus 20:8*

Safely through another week,
God has brought us on our way;
Let us now a blessing seek,
On th' approaching Sabbath-day:
Day of all the week the best,
Emblem of eternal rest.
—*John Newton, Olney Hymns, 1774[1]*

Presumably friendly discussions among professing Christians concerning the application of the fourth commandment often degenerate into confusion, accusations, criticisms, fear (of legalism by some and lawlessness by others), and even open hostility. One author describes the Sabbath controversy as "one of the family quarrels of longest standing."[2] Why is this so?

No other requirement among the Ten Commandments of Exodus 20 is as controversial in churches today as this one. Yes, it is true that people debate the use of the death penalty in connection with the sixth commandment, but no one suggests that we are free to murder someone if we feel like it.

No Christian approves of worshiping idols or disapproves of honoring parents. No brother or sister will accuse you of being legalistic if you're against stealing or are in favor of telling the truth. But I know many people who object to Sabbath keeping and approve of using the Lord's Day for work or personal pleasure. We don't argue about the other nine; why is the fourth commandment a catalyst for more heat than light?

The answer, I believe, is that many people approach the fourth commandment from the wrong direction. They are asking the wrong questions out of hearts that have wrong attitudes.[3]

This wrong attitude encourages a legalistic casuistry. Casuistry, from the Latin *casus,* is the attempt to apply general ethical and moral principles to particular cases of conscience and conduct. It is the effort to provide uniform, pat answers to every conceivable question of behavior.

The casuist wants to have everything he can and cannot

do in black and white, down to the smallest details of right and wrong. Sometimes the term is used prejudicially to suggest a dishonest or insincere manipulating of moral principles in order to justify behavior that is questionable. But there is surely nothing wrong and much that is right in wanting to understand how to apply biblical standards to specific life situations. We all need to be casuists in the good sense of understanding how to apply general biblical principles to the particular moral issues we face, but life isn't always as black and white as we would like.

Problems occur when we try to skip a step, when we rush to apply moral principles before we fully understand those principles. Instead of trying to identify in the Scriptures what the broad God-given purposes and functions of the Sabbath are, we tend to focus our attention on the narrow question of which activities are and are not permitted on the Lord's Day. We want to know in detail what we can *do* on the Sabbath before we have asked why we *have* a Sabbath. We ask such questions as, "Is it okay for my daughter to play soccer on Sunday? Am I breaking the Sabbath if I spend the afternoon catching up on business paperwork at home? And what about going out to a restaurant for dinner?"

Lawmakers in one of the New England colonies, in an effort to define which activities were and were not permitted on the Lord's Day, published thirty-nine pages of regulations, all in fine print! That, unfortunately, is representative of the way in which many have approached the whole issue of the Sabbath for centuries. "Let's skip the theoretical and theological and get right to the practical. I don't have time to study or think about the Lord's Day. Just give me a laminated, wallet-sized list of *do*s and *don't*s so I can get on with living."

That's the proverbial tail wagging the dog. Application must always be the servant of precept and principle. Theological shortcuts often lead to some kind of legalistic bondage. Instead of being, as John Newton called it, "day of all the week the best," Sunday has become, for some, day of all the week to dread. However, the Sabbath is not an oppressive, restrictive, or harsh master, as a common stereotype represents it to be. It may have become that historically, and it may still be that under some legalistic interpretations today; but it was not so in the design and intention of its Lord and Maker. Jesus, the Lord of the Sabbath, affirmed, "The Sabbath was made for man, not man for the Sabbath" (Mark 2:27).

The Sabbath was made in order to supply something that we as human beings need. It therefore exists in order to help us, not to hinder us. We think we have too much to do to take time to rest, but in truth we need what the Sabbath provides, and cannot do our work effectively without it. As Dorothy Bass rightly observes, "Whether we know the term *Sabbath* or not, we the harried citizens of late modernity yearn for the reality. We need Sabbath, even though we doubt that we have time for it."[4]

The Sabbath was not created to restrict us or burden us unduly. It is not a ball and chain forced upon us by an unloving tyrant. It is not an infringement of our liberty, as some think, but a pledge of true liberty under the sovereignty of God. Bass notes,

> For many of us, receiving this gift [of Sabbath] will require first discarding our image of Sabbath as a time of negative rules and restrictions, as a day of ob-

ligation (for Catholics) or a day without play (in memories of strict Protestant childhoods).[5]

The Sabbath existed from the beginning, exists now, and shall continue to exist until the end of the age as a weekly affirmation and celebration of God's sovereignty and of our true freedom under God's law.

GOD'S SOVEREIGNTY OVER TIME

The fourth commandment stands first of all as a declaration of God's sovereignty over time and over our use of God's time.

What is time? Augustine once responded to this question in a most interesting way: "If no one asks me, I know; if I wish to explain it to one who asks, I know not."[6]

We live in the element of time as a fish lives in water, but we do not sufficiently appreciate the fact that the Sabbath day and the weekly pattern of work and rest have their origin in God's work of creation. The commandment reminds us that "in six days the LORD made the heavens and the earth, the sea, and all that is in them, but he rested on the seventh day" (Exodus 20:11).

Time does not exist independently but is itself the product of God's creative power and purpose. Many scientists and historians are content to account for the division of time into years, seasons, months, and days on the basis of ancient observations of the cycles in nature. They imagine that ancient people observed that there were regular periods of warm, hot, cool, and cold weather during the year, and called them *seasons*.

Then other people noticed the changes in the shape of the moon. Someone recognized that the moon went through cycles of waxing (growing bigger) and waning (getting smaller). Thus there came to be *moonths* or *months*.

Another pattern was even more obvious. The sun always came up in the morning and went down in the evening. People called each of those periods a *day*.

But natural scientists and historians have no good explanation for the origin of the *week*. This is where their speculative theories disintegrate. Paul Jewett writes,

> The division of time into seven days in Israel remains a riddle, so far as historical explanation is concerned. There is no rhythm in nature, nor periodicity in the motion of the heavenly bodies, nor sequence in the patterns of ancient social behavior, which corresponds to the seven-day week.[7]

Historians are puzzled. There is no historical evidence for the origin of the week, they say, and of course that is true—if Scripture is rejected as a historical source of information. According to the Bible, we have the week because God ordained it, and indeed this is the origin of time and all its divisions. We read in Genesis,

> And God said, "Let there be light," and there was light. God saw that the light was good, and he separated the light from the darkness. God called the light "day," and the darkness he called "night." And there was evening, and there was morning—the first day. (Genesis 1:3–5)

Here we have the beginning of time. Where did it come from? God made it. As God created time by his great power, so he also determined its divisions. Here is the source of the sun and the moon and the times they define:

> And God said, "Let there be lights in the expanse of the sky to separate the day from the night, and let them serve as signs to mark seasons and days and years, and let them be lights in the expanse of the sky to give light on the earth." And it was so. God made two great lights—the greater light to govern the day and the lesser light to govern the night. He also made the stars. God set them in the expanse of the sky to give light on the earth, to govern the day and the night, and to separate light from darkness. And God saw that it was good. (vv. 14–18)

And the week:

> By the seventh day God had finished the work he had been doing; so on the seventh day he rested from all his work. And God blessed the seventh day and made it holy, because on it he rested from all the work of creating that he had done. (Genesis 2:2–3)

God blessed the seventh day and made it holy. Literally, that means that God sanctified it or *set it apart* (from the other days). God made the seventh day something special, a spiritual and material blessing for all humanity. Thus the seven-day cycle was born. The week was established by the sovereign appointment of the Creator, and from the very beginning God arranged the lives of his people around the Sabbath.

Because time belongs to the created order, man is subject to all of its limitations, and God is sovereign over it. All time belongs to the Creator, and he cannot be limited by it in any way. God is not tied to days, months, and years as we are. He does not grow older as we do. Time is something that is relevant to the created order, and we are subject to it because we are a part of creation, but God is not.

We are able to extend our working day by using electric lights, but we cannot extend the day. We cannot make it either longer or shorter. We are subject to time and have no authority over it. My digital watch goes right on flashing as a persistent reminder that God's time progresses independently of me and my wishes. No matter how hard I might try, I can't make tax day come later or Christmas come sooner. God made time, and his sovereignty over it is total.

When Joshua's hasty alliance with the Gibeonites was challenged by the Amorite alliance, he went out to meet the five kings in battle (Joshua 10:1–15). In the midst of the battle, Joshua pleaded with God to make the sun stand still, to extend the day so that he and his warriors could pursue their enemies. And God did it! The sun stood still at Gibeon; the moon stopped over the Valley of Aijalon, and the enemies of Joshua and the Lord were utterly defeated. "There has never been a day like it before or since, a day when the LORD listened to a man" (v. 14). That's the power of the God with whom we have to do!

When Hezekiah lay ill and dying, God told him that he would heal him and add fifteen years to his life. Hezekiah asked the Lord for a sign, some proof that he would indeed do as he had promised (2 Kings 20:1–11). In response to the king's request, the shadow went back ten steps. There is some question whether these ten steps were steps on a stairway in the palace (NIV) or degrees on the sundial of Ahaz (NKJV), but the point is that the lengthening shadow went back. God reversed time. We can't do that. We can change our clocks for daylight savings time, but we cannot really change time itself. Only God is sovereign over time.

Because all time is God's time, he has authority over our use of time. We are only stewards of God's time, and he commands a weekly cycle of work and rest.

Here is the offense of the Sabbath commandment. Ever since the Fall, when Adam and Eve declared their independence from God, everyone descending from our first parents has deeply resented God's claim of sovereignty over time. We think time is ours, to use as we please, and we do not respect the rule of the Eternal over the temporal.

GOD'S SOVEREIGNTY OVER WORK

Because God is sovereign over time, he is also sovereign over our work. "Six days you shall labor," he said. Many people assume that work is the result of the Fall—part of the curse—but that assumption is wrong. Before he even created the world, the Lord intended to employ both the man and the woman in the work of managing the earth.

> Then God said, "Let us make man in our image, in
> our likeness, and let them rule over the fish of the
> sea and the birds of the air, over the livestock, over

all the earth, and over all the creatures that move along the ground." So God created man in his own image, in the image of God he created him; male and female he created them. God blessed them and said to them, "Be fruitful and increase in number; fill the earth and subdue it. Rule over the fish of the sea and the birds of the air and over every living creature that moves on the ground." (Genesis 1:26–28)

When the Lord put Adam into the garden, he assigned him the task of cultivating it and taking care of it (Genesis 2:15). One of Adam's first jobs was to identify and classify all the different varieties of animals that God had made and that he, Adam, was now responsible to manage (vv. 19–20). One of the reasons for having Adam perform this task was to show him that there was no helper "suitable" for him in all of the animal kingdom (that is, no helper "comparable to him" [NKJV]). All of this was before the Fall of Genesis 3.

We were made to work. This is God's world and we are God's creation, bearing his image to imitate him in work and in rest. It is important that we understand this concept because we live in a society where many deny both the importance and the meaningfulness of work.

We live in a world where people think that the less work you can do, the better off you are. But God, who made the world, says that the meaning of our existence is inseparable from the work we do. To deny the importance of work is to deny ourselves and eventually to destroy ourselves.

The fourth commandment asserts that work is a person's faithful response to the word of God. All honest work is therefore a spiritual vocation and has meaning. This is true whether my field of labor is the Scripture or the soil, whether I'm a missionary or I work at McDonald's. We have lost the concept of all work being a calling. We think that pastors and missionaries are called, but that other people merely find jobs.

A dualism permeates our thinking, separating the sacred from the secular. Preaching is obviously a sacred work to be done to the glory of God. But ordinary work like plowing dirt, pounding nails, sweeping floors, or selling lipstick is considered secular. Anybody can do it. However, the fourth commandment brings all work under the immediate authority of the Lord and renders every legitimate vocation an opportunity to glorify him. Pounding nails to the glory of God is a sacred calling. This is the distinctively biblical view of work.

The effects of the Fall were to introduce pain, hardship, and frustration into every work. The very ground itself is cursed because of our sin. The whole creation groans and suffers from its slavery to corruption (Romans 8:20–22). As a fallen race we find that our work is difficult: the ground produces both wheat and weeds, and even our wages perish with our death.

In redemption, the new creation, Jesus Christ restores humanity to a proper view of work. We are again enabled by God's grace to understand the importance of work as being an obedient response to God.

There were some believers in Thessalonica who maintained that Christ had brought an end to the cycle of work and rest. They believed that they had entered into their rest and had only to wait for his coming again. That sounded very spiritual, but it had some problems—they got hungry while they were waiting. So they appealed to their brothers and sisters in the church who didn't share their views to share their hard-earned bread with them. They essentially expected to live off the labors of others, as parasites feed off their hosts.

Paul wrote to the Thessalonians in order to correct this gross distortion and misapplication of the truth. He told them to "keep away from every brother who is idle and does not live according to the teaching you received from us," and to enforce the principle that "if a man will not work, he shall not eat" (2 Thessalonians 3:6, 10). Such persons Paul commanded with apostolic authority "to settle down and earn the bread they eat" (v. 12). In Christ, then, work is an essential part of the will of God.

GOD'S SOVEREIGNTY OVER REST

The fourth commandment also declares God's sovereignty over rest: "Six days you shall labor and do all your work, but the seventh day is a Sabbath to the LORD your God. On it you shall not do any work" (Exodus 20:9–10). The Sabbath was appointed to be a day of rest. Because God rested, humans, made in God's image, should also rest. The Sabbath was not oppressive; it was, and is, a blessing.

"The LORD blessed the Sabbath day and made it holy" (v. 11). Some people think of the Sabbath as the Jewish day of rest, but in blessing the Sabbath, God ordained it to be a celebration for all of creation. He provided rest for parents, children, servants, guests, and visitors—and even livestock.

Indeed, even the land itself was to enjoy a Sabbath rest every seventh year, when the fields were to lie fallow and unplanted (Leviticus 25:1–5).

The Sabbath is God's appointed holiday. The King of the universe gives all his subjects one day off every week to celebrate his creation, to interrupt their daily work and to rest in his, and thereby to be refreshed. One of the sweetest blessings of the Sabbath is refreshment.

> Six days do your work, but on the seventh day do not work, so that your ox and your donkey may rest and the slave born in your household, and the alien as well, may be refreshed. (Exodus 23:12)

Moses assembled the whole Israelite community and said to them,

> These are the things the LORD has commanded you to do: For six days, work is to be done, but the seventh day shall be your holy day, a Sabbath of rest ["complete rest," NASB] to the LORD. (Exodus 35:1–2)

> Six days you shall labor and do all your work, but the seventh day is a Sabbath to the LORD your God. On it you shall not do any work, neither you, nor your son or daughter, nor your manservant or maidservant, nor your ox, your donkey or any of your animals, nor the alien within your gates, so that your manservant and maidservant may rest, as you do. (Deuteronomy 5:13–14)

In the Sabbath, God gave us all a holy day (or, holiday). When the government gives us a holiday, we rejoice. That's good news! We don't have to go to school or the office! We can relax! I've never known anyone to complain about not having to work on the Fourth of July or Labor Day.

However, when *God* says, "I am going to give you a holiday," people actually grumble and complain. They don't want that holiday. They would rather work. Suddenly, "time is money," and we don't want to lose all that Sunday business. We don't want to waste our time resting, relaxing, and enjoying the Lord and his works. We have our own work to do.

Rebellious people do not want to rest in God's work or celebrate his creation. Like our first parents, we each want to be our own god. We want to rest in our own works and celebrate our own accomplishments.

The "natural man" imagines that he is divine, and believes in his ability to save himself by his own work. Thus, he actually resents God's interruption of his work. He prefers to become a slave to his work, convincing himself that what he does is all that holds the world, or at least the company, together. This is not dedication, but destruction. The nation will not collapse because we take a day off. Even the president goes to Camp David now and then to relax and enjoy himself.

God has, since the completion of creation, guaranteed us a day when we can be refreshed both physically and spiritually. We need it. That's pretty obvious, isn't it? Stress is a major issue in health care today. It is literally killing us. Some degree of stress is unavoidable, necessary, and even beneficial. But prolonged stress takes its toll on both body and soul. We need the rest and refreshment that God has provided for us in the Sabbath blessing.

The Sabbath calls me to recognize that the world doesn't depend on me. The planet is not going to fall apart if I don't go to the office, make some phone calls, or get this or that done today. Somehow God seems to keep the universe going without my help. We can pause from our labors and rest in his, realizing that in the end it is God who holds it all together, "sustaining all things by his powerful word" (Hebrews 1:3). It truly is a day for celebration!

> This is the day the Lord has made;
>   let us rejoice and be glad in it.
>   (Psalm 118:24)

REVIEW

1. Why do friendly discussions of the fourth commandment often become heated?
2. What is casuistry? Is casuistry good or bad?
3. Why do we often have problems applying biblical principles concerning the Sabbath to our lives?
4. How do theological shortcuts produce legalistic bondage?
5. How is the Sabbath an affirmation of God's sovereignty over time?
6. How do some people explain the origin of time and its divisions from nature? What is the biblical explanation?
7. How did the week originate? Is there any natural explanation for the week?

8. Are there limitations on God's sovereignty over time?

9. Why does the fourth commandment offend some people?

10. How is the Sabbath an affirmation of God's sovereignty over our work?

11. Is work a consequence of humanity's fall into sin?

12. What is the dualism that permeates our thinking? How does it affect our thinking about work?

13. How is the Sabbath an affirmation of God's sovereignty over rest?

14. What does it mean to rest? How can rest be a celebration?

15. Why doesn't everyone want to rest and celebrate on the Sabbath?

RESPONSE

1. Do I argue with others about the Sabbath? Why?

2. Am I a casuist? In what sense? Do I tend to answer a question without going through the sometimes lengthy process that leads to the correct answer?

3. How much of my thinking about the Sabbath is based on Scripture, and how much of it is influenced by the culture and society in which I live?

4. Have I ever heard any sermons on the Sabbath? Who preached them and when?

5. Dorothy Bass says, "We need Sabbath." Do *I* need Sabbath? Why or why not?

6. What are the implications for me of the fact that time is created? What are the implications for God?

7. If I am a steward of time under God, am I as careful with time as I am with money? Why or why not?

8. Is my attitude toward work biblical? If not, how does it need to change?

9. How does the sacred/secular dualism affect my thinking? In what specific areas is it evident?

10. Why do I feel guilty when I rest? How should I feel?

THREE

SABBATH OR LORD'S DAY?
OLD TESTAMENT ROOTS

Remember the Sabbath day by keeping it holy.
Six days you shall labor and do all your work,
but the seventh day is a Sabbath to the LORD your God.
—*Exodus 20:8–10*

New graces ever gaining
From this our day of rest,
We reach the rest remaining
To spirits of the blest.
To Holy Ghost be praises,
To Father, and to Son;
The church her voice upraises
To thee, blest Three in One.
—*Christopher Wordsworth, 1862*

We have noted that much discussion of the fourth commandment is marked by confusion and controversy. J. Douma laments that "throughout European, British, and American Protestantism, rather sharp polemics have been waged about the Sabbath question, so sharp that at times a church split appeared inevitable."[1] Not only have some churches become divided over the Sabbath issue, but so have some families! Dutch theologian A. van Selms wrote some years ago that ten thousand families in the Netherlands alone experienced serious quarrels over what activities were and were not permissible on Sunday.[2] Some of this confusion is the fruit of misinformation or a lack of information. Many people try to proceed to the details of Sabbath observance without first of all establishing the true meaning of the Sabbath. As R. J. Rushdoony reminds us, "The shifting of emphasis from the meaning of the Sabbath to quibbling about regulations for the Sabbath is certainly no honor to the Sabbath."[3]

Two equally great and destructive dangers that we must avoid when talking about the Sabbath are legalism and lawlessness. First, we must avoid binding our consciences (and the consciences of others) to rules and regulations that are not lawful, that is, not required by the Word of God. A misplaced zeal that goes beyond the teaching of Scripture always turns liberty into legalism.

Second, we must also avoid the danger of freeing our consciences from what is required by the Word of God. A misguided liberality that falls short of the teaching of Scripture through laxness always turns liberty into license.

In this chapter we will continue to survey biblical teaching concerning the Sabbath. We want to consider its past,

present, and future, and especially identify the broad purposes and functions of this special day. Before we can meaningfully discuss specific behavior or activities on the Sabbath,
we need to understand the general purposes for which God
ordained it in the first place.

Theologians sometimes speak of the organic and progressive character of biblical revelation.[4] By this they simply
mean that just as an acorn grows and develops into a mature
oak tree, so concepts that are introduced in seed form in
early revelation (such as Genesis) grow and develop pro-
gressively throughout the Old Testament Scriptures until
they come to full flower and fruit in the New Testament. The
oak tree, while different in form from the acorn, is not different in essence. What the oak tree has become was implicit
(or hidden) in the acorn, and the promise of the acorn is ex-
plicit (or clearly seen) in the more fully developed oak. Similarly, the New Testament revelation is concealed in the Old,
and the Old Testament is revealed in the New.[5]

We can distinguish in the Scriptures four distinct stages
of Sabbath revelation: the Creation Sabbath, the Exodus
Sabbath, the Resurrection Sabbath, and the Final Sabbath.
The first two stages are the Old Testament roots, and the last
two are the New Testament flower and fruit.

THE CREATION SABBATH

The fourth commandment begins with the words, *"Remember* the Sabbath day by keeping it holy" (Exodus 20:8).
Some people insist that the observance of a weekly Sabbath
day originated in the book of Exodus, but the word *remember*

does not introduce something that is brand new to the people; it directs them to recall something out of their past. How much in the past? Some would suggest the very recent past, such as the account of the Exodus event (see Exodus 16:22–30). However, the text says to look further: "For in six days the LORD made the heavens and the earth, the sea, and all that is in them, but he rested on the seventh day. Therefore the LORD blessed the Sabbath day and made it holy" (Exodus 20:11). *Remember* reaches all the way back to the time of creation, to the very beginning of time.

The idea of the Sabbath, therefore, did not originate with any man, or any group of men, but with God. This is very important for us to recognize. The Sabbath is not Moses' Sabbath, as some seem to think. Nor is it Israel's holy day, as others insist. Rather, it is God's Sabbath, God's holy day. He is the one who brought it into being, and he is the one who is honored by it.

When the heavens and the earth were completed, God "rested from all his work" and invited the man and the woman to join him in his celebration of, and satisfaction in, what he had made. He "blessed" the day and "made it holy," and both of those expressions have specific reference to humanity (Genesis 2:1–3).

God did not bless the day for his own sake, but for the man and woman he had created on the sixth day. The Sabbath was appointed for their benefit—for their happiness, joy, and refreshment. So Jesus declared, "The Sabbath was made for man" (Mark 2:27). It is possible to translate this sentence as "The Sabbath came into being for the sake of man" (NASB margin), thus directing us back to the original institution and intention of the Sabbath. It was not for

God—he didn't need to rest or be refreshed. He wasn't tired after six days of creating; nor did God need to pause and catch his breath. The Sabbath was God's gift to the man and woman he had prepared to be his servants and workers on the earth.

He blessed the day and sanctified it ("made it holy"). That is, he set it apart from the other days of the week and made it a holy day. Thus, the Sabbath was not simply to be a day off from work. The reason for taking time off from work was to celebrate God's great power and authority that had so recently been demonstrated in the creation of the heavens and the earth. "The earth is the LORD'S, and everything in it, the world, and all who live in it; for he founded it upon the seas and established it upon the waters" (Psalm 24:1–2). In the Sabbath, the sovereign Lord invites Adam and Eve and all their posterity to join him in a special day of celebration. Why would anyone object to receiving an invitation to a party—a holy party?

The Sabbath was intended to be a day of rest from doing work in order to be free to perform spiritual acts of worship and service. The first question of the Westminster Shorter Catechism asks, "What is the chief end of man?" It answers, "Man's chief end is to glorify God, and to enjoy him forever." When do we get to enjoy God? We don't have to wait until we enter glory to joyfully serve him. We can and do enjoy him every day. But sometimes our days are so full and our work is so frustrating that our days are not very enjoyable. God gives us the Sabbath as a day when we can pause from our work and turn our whole attention to our Creator as the source of our life, breath, and refreshment. F. N. Lee observes, "God therefore intended the sabbath to be the means of producing spiritual fruitfulness in the lives of His people, and to be the *dominating* factor in their lives."[6]

Because the Sabbath begins in Genesis 1 and 2, it is a creation ordinance.[7] Like marriage and work, the Sabbath was ordained before the Fall, for all people of all time. It cannot be confined to the ceremonial law appointed specifically for the nation of Israel, but was intended to be a celebration of creation for Adam and all his posterity. John Murray notes, "Since the action of God in creation has relevance quite apart from sin or redemption, we are bound to conclude that the sabbath institution would have had relevance to Adam in his state of innocence."[8]

Is there any historical evidence to indicate that the Sabbath was ever observed before the Exodus? Some argue that the silence of Genesis concerning Sabbath observance indicates that there was no weekly Sabbath in patriarchal times, and that Israel began observing the Sabbath only after the Exodus. Murray responds with bristling brevity, "Genesis is not silent."[9] Lee devotes over eighty pages to a detailed discussion of Sabbath keeping from Adam to Moses,[10] concluding,

> The sabbath is in the Decalogue; but it is in the Decalogue because it had been before both in human nature and in history. Thus human nature, history and Scripture are all in alliance under God; all demand a sabbath, and all point to the sabbath.[11]

There is also evidence of the importance of a seven-day pattern in other cultures, although the pattern is corrupted. We would expect it to be corrupted because of the Fall.

The Babylonians, for example, celebrated every seventh day of the months Elul and Marcheshwan. The seventh, fourteenth, twenty-first, and twenty-eighth days were all special days of penitence and prayer. But, unlike the biblical Sabbath celebration, the Babylonian seventh days were perceived to be unlucky days. These days, called *shappatu,* were bad days. People didn't go to work or travel on *shappatu* because they feared that if they did, everything that could go wrong would go wrong. Consider some of the rules that applied to the Babylonian *shappatu:*

> The shepherd of the great peoples shall not eat flesh cooked on coals or baked bread. He shall not put on clean (clothes). He shall not bring an offering. The king shall not travel by chariot. He shall not speak as ruler. At the place of the mystery the one who views the sacrifices shall not utter a word. The physician shall not lay his hands on a patient. (The day) is not suitable for carrying out plans. At night the king shall bring his gift to the great gods; he shall offer a sacrifice; the lifting up of his hands is then acceptable to the god.[12]

Only among biblical people has one day in seven been a holy day of rest in, and celebration of, the person and works of God.

THE EXODUS SABBATH

Next in the progress of revelation is the Sabbath as it was observed in Israel: the Exodus Sabbath ("Exodus" here refers to the event rather than the book by that name). The Exodus Sabbath gathers up the essence of the Creation Sabbath and adds something more to it.

In the "Second Law" (Deuteronomy), the Ten Commandments are repeated, but the wording of the fourth commandment begins differently than in Exodus 20. The difference is significant. Here the commandment begins, "Observe the Sabbath day by keeping it holy" (Deuteronomy 5:12). The first word is not "remember," as in Exodus, but "observe."

The next section has very similar language establishing a pattern of six days of work followed by "a Sabbath to the LORD your God" that extends to the family, livestock, aliens, and servants.

But then there follows a very striking addition to the fourth commandment:

> Remember that you were slaves in Egypt and that the LORD your God brought you out of there with a mighty hand and an outstretched arm. Therefore the LORD your God has commanded you to observe the Sabbath day. (Deuteronomy 5:15)

What's the point of this additional statement? The point is that now there are two things that the Sabbath is to commemorate:

1. In six days the Lord, as Creator, made the heavens and the earth.
2. God's people were slaves in the land of Egypt, and the Lord, as Savior, delivered them in a mighty act of redemption.

The Exodus Sabbath, then, is a celebration of creation and, additionally, a celebration of the redemption accomplished by God's great power in the Exodus event. The original creation ordinance is not abrogated by the new wording, but is actually expanded.

Thus the Sabbath became *a sign of the covenant*, an emblem of the special relationship of grace between the Redeemer-God and his chosen people.

> Then the LORD said to Moses, "Say to the Israelites, 'You must observe my Sabbaths. This will be a sign between me and you for the generations to come, so you may know that I am the LORD, who makes you holy.
>
> " 'Observe the Sabbath, because it is holy to you. Anyone who desecrates it must be put to death; whoever does any work on that day must be cut off from his people. For six days, work is to be done, but the seventh day is a Sabbath of rest, holy to the LORD. Whoever does any work on the Sabbath day must be put to death. The Israelites are to observe the Sabbath, celebrating it for the generations to come as a lasting covenant. It will be a sign between me and the Israelites forever, for in six days the LORD made the heavens and the earth, and on the seventh day he abstained from work and rested.' " (Exodus 31:12–17)

There are two things here that we need to recognize. All people are required to acknowledge God as their Creator, and thus all are obligated to keep the Creation Sabbath. But only Israel knew him as the Redeemer. Thus, the Sabbath that was appointed as a celebration of creation for all humanity took on a special meaning to Israel as God's covenant people. The Sabbath became a sign of redemption or a new creation. It did not begin that way, but the Sabbath became a sign to remind Israel that God had by grace sanctified, chosen, and delivered them.

The Exodus Sabbath, like the Creation Sabbath, was to be a day of holy rest and celebration. Work was forbidden in order to guarantee a day for rest and refreshment of both body and soul. The people on that day were to celebrate God's works of creation and redemption. The Sabbath was appointed to be a sign. As a sign of creation, the Sabbath testifies that the world depends upon God, not man, for its continued existence. As a sign of grace, the Sabbath declares that salvation depends upon the power of God and not human works.

Anyone who worked on the Sabbath day effectively denied that God is the Creator and symbolically rejected salvation by grace. He was a covenant-breaker, and as such God commanded that he should be put to death (Exodus 31:14). This was to show everyone in the covenant community of Israel that the penalty for rejecting God and his grace is always death.

The Sabbath was to be a holy day. The number of sacrifices in the tabernacle (later the temple) were doubled (morning and evening), and worship became a prominent part of the entire day (Numbers 28:1–10; see also 1 Chronicles 16:39–40).[13]

It is important to recognize that the Sabbath we're talking about was not like the Jewish Sabbath we meet later in the Gospels. The attitude of godly people toward the Sabbath in the Old Testament was considerably different from that of the Pharisees in Jesus' day. By then the rabbis had twisted celebration into mourning, and freedom into bondage. This disguised and distorted Sabbath bore little resemblance to the day of praise, melody, and song it once had been.

Biblical literature prior to the disastrous times of exile and captivity to Assyria and Babylonia reveals the heartfelt conviction of many people:

> It is good to praise the LORD
>> and make music to your name, O Most High,
> to proclaim your love in the morning
>> and your faithfulness at night,
> to the music of the ten-stringed lyre
>> and the melody of the harp.
> For you make me glad by your deeds, O LORD;
>> I sing for joy at the works of your hands.
> How great are your works, O LORD,
>> how profound your thoughts!
>> (Psalm 92:1–5)

Significantly, this particular psalm is titled "A psalm. A song. For the Sabbath day." Does the psalmist sound oppressed, burdened, or in any way unhappy because it is the Sabbath? The Sabbath in the Old Testament was a day for *rejoicing*. Many modern readers of the Bible seem to miss this. They imagine the Old Testament Sabbath as an oppressive day burdened by endless rules and prohibitions. But it wasn't like that! People didn't have to go to work! They were given an opportunity to gather with their families and friends from morning till evening and enjoy the presence of God! It was a *good* day—one in which they could play lively tunes on their harps and sing joyful psalms from their hearts.

But by Jesus' day this joyful Sabbath had become corrupted, probably under the influence of the Exile. When the Jews were taken from the Promised Land to places like Assyria and Babylonia, they met people who viewed the seventh day as an unlucky day in which no one dared to do anything because "it would only turn out wrong." That negative view probably affected the attitude of the displaced Jews toward their own Sabbath celebration.

Evolving rabbinical oral traditions, eventually compiled in written form in the Talmud about the year 200, attempted to provide specific legal regulation of Jewish life.[14] The rabbis formulated hundreds of regulations identifying in great detail what constituted work on the Sabbath, and it was this restrictive, binding, man-made Sabbath that Jesus confronted so forcefully. We will look at Jesus' conflict with the Pharisees later,[15] but keep in mind that the Exodus Sabbath was a joyful celebration of both creation and redemption.

Creation and redemption. These two themes bored deep into the soil of the Hebrew Scriptures and were the roots that fed and sustained the body of Sabbath revelation that would produce flower and fruit in the New Testament.

REVIEW

1. How do misinformation and a lack of information about the Sabbath fuel controversy within many churches and families?
2. What must we understand before we can meaningfully discuss how to keep the Sabbath?

3. What are some dangers that we must avoid when talking about the Sabbath?

4. What is meant by "the organic and progressive nature of biblical revelation?"

5. What are the four stages of Sabbath revelation?

6. Who celebrated the first Sabbath?

7. What was the first Sabbath intended to celebrate?

8. What is a creation ordinance? How do creation ordinances differ from the laws given to Israel?

9. Is there any evidence that the Sabbath was observed by people before the Exodus?

10. What was the character of Babylonian seventh days?

11. What revelatory content did the Exodus Sabbath add to the Creation Sabbath?

12. How is the Sabbath a sign of the covenant between God and his elect people?

13. Why was it decreed that someone who worked on the Sabbath should be put to death?

14. Were Old Testament believers unhappy when it was the Sabbath?

15. What is the Talmud and how did it originate?

16. Was the Sabbath kept by the Pharisees in the same way it was kept by believing Jews in the Old Testament? If not, how was it different?

RESPONSE

1. What is legalism? What is lawlessness? How successfully have I avoided these two destructive dangers in my life? How can I avoid them?

2. How do I *remember* the Sabbath day? What if, on this day, I thought about all that God has done for me and for all those who have gone before me? How would that change my week?

3. How often do I reflect upon the truth that God is my Creator? What are the implications of that biblical teaching for my life?

4. F. N. Lee says that God intended the Sabbath to be the *dominating* factor in our lives. What influence does the Sabbath have on my life from day to day and week to week?

5. How is the Sabbath a symbol of God's grace in redemption to me?

6. Psalm 92 is a song for the Sabbath. What does it reveal about the hearts of those who sang it? Have I misjudged the depth of spirituality within Old Testament believers?

7. Old Testament saints celebrated creation and redemption on the Sabbath day. What do *I* celebrate on the Lord's Day?

FOUR

SABBATH OR LORD'S DAY?
NEW TESTAMENT
FLOWER AND FRUITS

There remains, then, a Sabbath-rest
for the people of God.
—*Hebrews 4:9*

Come, let us join with one accord
In hymns around the throne:
This is the day our rising Lord
Hath made and called his own.
This is the day that God hath blessed,
The brightest of the sev'n,
Type of that everlasting rest
The saints enjoy in heav'n.
—*Charles Wesley, 1763*

What is the relationship between the Old Testament Sabbath and the Lord's Day, the first day of the week, when Christians in the New Testament met for worship?

On the surface, the differences are great enough that some people think there is no relationship between them at all! But when we consider the organic and progressive nature of biblical revelation, we are not surprised to discover that the Sabbath and the Lord's Day are one in essence, just as the acorn and the oak are one, even though they differ in form.

What the Lord's Day has become was implicit in the Sabbath, and the promise of the Sabbath is most clearly seen in the Lord's Day.

We have considered the Old Testament roots of the Sabbath. Now let us look at the New Testament flower and fruits, the Resurrection Sabbath and the Final Sabbath.

THE RESURRECTION SABBATH

The Resurrection Sabbath (or Christian Sabbath) gathers up the meanings of both the Creation Sabbath and the Exodus Sabbath, and transforms them into a celebration of Jesus' resurrection from the dead. The Sabbath in the New Testament thus becomes a sign of a new creation completed and a greater redemption accomplished. It becomes a sign of the New Covenant, ratified by the blood of Jesus.

The relationship between the Old Covenant and the New Covenant is characterized by both unity and diversity. We should not be surprised that this is so. The whole Old Covenant economy looks forward to, and anticipates, the works of God that are celebrated as accomplishments in the New Covenant.

The Old Covenant sign of circumcision is transformed into the New Covenant sign of baptism.[1] The Old Covenant Passover is transformed into the New Covenant Lord's Supper (Luke 22:7–20 and parallel passages; see also 1 Corinthians 5:6–8). The Old Covenant temple is transformed into the New Covenant temple: "You also, like living stones, are being built into a spiritual house to be a holy priesthood" (1 Peter 2:5; see also 1 Corinthians 3:16). And the Old Covenant Sabbath is transformed into the New Covenant Sabbath (or Lord's Day) by the resurrection of the Lord of the Sabbath from the dead.[2]

The New Covenant certainly introduces significant changes in the application or practice of the fourth commandment, but the one who provides continuity from old to new is Jesus Christ, "the same yesterday and today and forever" (Hebrews 13:8). As Creator, he blessed the Sabbath and made it holy. As Redeemer, he appointed it to be a sign of the covenant of his grace. The Sabbath is now, and always has been, the Lord's Day![3]

In Mark 2, Jesus makes a statement that is definitive for our understanding of the relationship between the Old Covenant Sabbath and the New Covenant Lord's Day. He says, "The Son of Man is Lord even of the Sabbath" (v. 28).

Don't fail to see what Jesus reveals here concerning himself and his relationship to the Sabbath. Jesus is one with the LORD (Jehovah) who gave the Sabbath; indeed, he is Jehovah incarnate.

When Moses asked God how he should respond to the enslaved Israelites if they asked him the name of the God who sent him, God said to Moses, "I AM WHO I AM. This is what you are to say to the Israelites: 'I AM has sent me to you' " (Exodus 3:14).

Jesus also identified himself as "I AM." He told the Jews, "Your father Abraham rejoiced at the thought of seeing my day; he saw it and was glad." Indeed, "before Abraham was born, I AM!" (John 8:56, 58, small caps added). The Jews who were present understood exactly what he meant. They picked up stones to stone him because they rightly recognized that he was claiming to be the LORD of the Old Testament; he was claiming to be God.

As Lord of the Sabbath, Jesus claims continuity with the Sabbath. That means, then, that it was Jesus who instituted the Creation Sabbath. And it was Jesus who sanctified the Exodus Sabbath and appointed it as a covenant sign.

The Old Testament Sabbath was Jesus' day: it was the Lord's Day. The meaning of the Sabbath has always been the same: true rest can only be found in Christ. Throughout the Old Testament, there was an earnest longing for rest among the saints of God. Noah's father called him Noah (meaning "rest" in Hebrew) in the hope that "this one shall give us rest from our work" (Genesis 5:29 NASB).[4] But Noah wasn't the one who could provide rest for God's people; believers had to continue looking for the promise of God.

True rest would come in the fullness of time, when the promise was fulfilled in the person of God's Son. Jesus cried out,

> Come to me, all you who are weary and burdened, and I will give you rest. Take my yoke upon you and learn from me, for I am gentle and humble in heart,

and you will find rest for your souls. For my yoke is easy and my burden is light. (Matthew 11:28–30)

How does this relate to the Sabbath? The word translated "rest" in this passage is not the word *Sabbath*, but what *is* interesting is this: when the Greek-speaking Jews translated the Hebrew Old Testament into Greek, they didn't translate the word *Sabbath;* rather, they transliterated it, coining a new word, *sabbaton,* for *Sabbath*. And when they were asked, "What in the world does *sabbaton* mean," they answered, *"Sabbaton* means *anapausis"* (from which we get the word *pause*).

The word that Jesus uses here is *anapausis,* a synonym for *Sabbath*. Jesus therefore is saying, "The rest that was promised, which you have looked for in Creation and the Exodus, can only be found in me. Come to me, all you who are weary and burdened, and I will give it to you."

When did he do that? Jesus rose on the first day of the week. On that Sunday morning he completed a new creation, accomplished a new and full redemption, and sanctified by his resurrection a new day for the celebration of the New Covenant. His people can rest in the fullness and finality of what Jesus did.

Demonstrating the greatness of Jesus' power to save, the Spirit was given while the believers were together on the Day of Pentecost. People today are often so distracted by the phenomenon of tongues in Acts 2 that they fail to appreciate the spiritual significance of this singular event. Pentecost was not something brand new. In fact, it was the occasion for bringing "God-fearing Jews from every nation under heaven" (v. 5) to Jerusalem.

Why were they there? Pentecost, also known as the Feast of Weeks, was celebrated seven weeks after the first day of the Feast of Unleavened Bread, or the fiftieth day after Passover.[5] The Feast of Weeks was an opportunity for God's people to express joy and thanksgiving to him for the firstfruits of the wheat harvest, much as in America we celebrate Thanksgiving on the fourth Thursday in November each year.

Do you see? Pentecost for the Christian is not a celebration of tongues. It's about the success of evangelism and missions, the triumph of the gospel as it penetrates and conquers the nations. Pentecost celebrates the firstfruits of the worldwide spiritual harvest of the risen Lord Jesus. On the Pentecost after Christ our Passover was sacrificed for us, the promise of an abundant harvest was displayed in a demonstration of tongues[6] and by the conversion of some three thousand people, representing every nation under heaven.

What day of the week was Pentecost? Like the day of our Lord's resurrection, it was the first day of the week.[7] Here is a twofold confirmation of the change of the holy day: Christ arose and the Spirit was given on the first day of the week. Christopher Wordsworth sees three spotlights aimed at Sunday:

> On thee, at the creation, The light first had its
> birth;
> On thee, for our salvation, Christ rose from depths
> of earth;
> On thee our Lord, victorious, The Spirit sent from
> heav'n;
> And thus on thee, most glorious, A triple light was
> giv'n.[8]

The first day of the week is the Resurrection rest, the New Covenant Sabbath.[9]

The biblical evidence seems clear that the infant church in the New Testament held Sunday in great honor. Our Lord rose on the first day. Many of his postresurrection appearances to various witnesses also occurred on Sundays.[10] After the Resurrection, in striking contrast to their previous practice, Jesus' disciples habitually met and worshiped on the first day of the week. Offerings to help the poor among God's people were to be collected "on the first day of every week" (1 Corinthians 16:1–4) because that was when the church met regularly in their devotion to apostolic teaching, fellowship, prayer, and communion. This instruction was not specific to the Corinthians, for Paul says, "Do what I told the Galatian churches to do." En route to Jerusalem for the last time, the apostle Paul tarried in Troas for a whole week so that he could preach and break bread with the church on Sunday. He left as soon as the all-night service was over (Acts 20:6–11). The revelation that the apostle John received and recorded was given to him "on the Lord's Day" (Revelation 1:10).

All of this leads R. T. Beckwith to observe,

> It is a striking fact that the Jewish sabbath almost disappears from recorded Christian practice after Christ's resurrection. The very day before his resurrection occurs, we find the disciples resting on the Jewish sabbath (Luke 23:56; cp. also Mark 16:1; John 19:42), but after it has happened the observance of the seventh day is never mentioned except as a tolerated option for Jewish Christians (Rom. 14:5), or

an intolerable imposition by Judaising heretics (Gal. 4:9–11; Col. 2:16f.), or in passages where Paul reasons with the Jews in the synagogue on the sabbath (Acts 13:14, 42, 44; 17:2; 18:4; cp. also Acts 16:13), not apparently because the observance of the day is a regular part of his own devotional practice but because it provides an excellent opportunity for evangelism.[11]

In imitation of apostolic practice, we also gather on the first day of the week to celebrate the resurrection of our Lord from the dead and to find our rest in the work he has done.

THE FINAL SABBATH

The Resurrection Sabbath is not the final rest. There remains a Sabbath rest for the people of God that is yet to come, the Final Sabbath. Just as the Lord's Supper combines elements of memorial and expectation—remembering his death and anticipating his coming[12]—so the Lord's Day gathers up all that has gone before and looks for that which is yet to come.

The Spirit speaks of the Final Sabbath in Hebrews 4.[13] This chapter is intended to be a warning. Many people who had the good news preached to them while wandering in the desert (that is, the Exodus) failed to enter into the rest promised by God because of their disobedience (v. 6). They had sinful, unbelieving hearts that turned away from the living God (3:12), and the word they heard was of no value to them because it was not united or combined with faith (4:2).

Their example of failing to enter Canaan shows us that we also can come close to the rest promised by God without actually obtaining it. There is a way to hell, even from the very gate of heaven. The *profession* of faith is not the same as the *possession* of faith.

Chantry rightly calls attention to the fact that the rest in view is *God's* rest.[14] The personal pronouns employed by the author are clear and emphatic: "They shall never enter *my* rest" (Hebrews 3:11), "*his* rest" (v. 18), "*his* rest" (4:1), "*that* rest" and "*my* rest" (v. 3), "*my* rest" (v. 5), and "*that* rest" (v. 11). The NIV translators also insert "rest" in 4:6 and "God's" in 4:10 to help the reader follow the point of the passage more clearly.

The point is that rest in general is not the goal, nor is the goal for man to enter into a rest that is the fruit of his own accomplishments. God's rest is the only rest there is, and the only way to enter God's rest is through the finished work of Jesus Christ. What is the nature of this rest which "we who have believed enter" (Hebrews 4:3), but which some people will never enter because of disobedience? Chantry explains.

> The chief issue is not non-activity on God's part but full enjoyment of his work and the receiving of glory from the work of his hands. However, he did not intend to enter this rest alone. From the seventh day of creation, man has been called into God's rest. Man is to share with God the pleasure and satisfaction of all God's work. Man is to glorify God, not for some future personal blessing but for God's finished work. Man is to be God's special companion in the enjoy-

ment of God's finished work and in giving God glory for his finished work.[15]

Those who entered the land with Joshua obtained only a symbol of the rest that God promised, "for if Joshua had given them rest, God would not have spoken later about another day" (Hebrews 4:8).

The author's point is that there *remains* a Sabbath rest for the people of God. Douma observes,

> The weekly Sabbath was a sign of the eternal Sabbath. That feature applies just as well to Sunday. The definitive rest from our works, similar to God's rest from His work, is not yet within our reach (Heb. 4:9–10). *Both* the Sabbath and Sunday are a sign pointing to that truth.[16]

We must be diligent to enter that rest, holding firmly until the end the confidence in Jesus Christ that we had at the beginning. For such lifelong perseverance, we need regular and frequent encouragement from our fellow believers (Hebrews 3:13–14; see also 10:25).

Sunday, then, is a celebration of the resurrection of Christ, an anticipation of our resurrection in him, and a God-given opportunity to encourage one another in his grace. Christ is coming again to bring final salvation and rest to all who eagerly await him. By faith we long and look for that day, and we must also prepare for it. That final rest will only be obtained by those who persevere in their faith and obedience to the living Christ.

The book of Revelation is a book of encouragement and

hope because it enables us to peer into the Final Sabbath, which has no end. Those who worship the beast and his image have no rest, day or night, and "the smoke of their torment rises for ever and ever." Entering God's rest "calls for patient endurance on the part of the saints who obey God's commandments and remain faithful to Jesus." In the end, says the Spirit, "they will rest from their labor, for their deeds will follow them" (Revelation 14:9–13).

Continuing to be faithful to Jesus in this life requires, among other things, obeying God's commandments—including the command to remember the Sabbath day by keeping it holy. Although the day of the week and some aspects of the manner of celebrating the day have been changed by the Lord of the Sabbath, the New Testament does not abrogate Sabbath keeping as such. In fact, it requires it.

The author of Hebrews insists, "There remains, then, a Sabbath-rest for the people of God" (4:9). The word translated "Sabbath-rest"[17] is an unusual Greek word that is used only here in the New Testament. The cognate verb, however, is used several times in the Greek translation of the Old Testament, the Septuagint.[18] There it consistently serves as a descriptive term for observing or keeping the Sabbath. Stephen M. Baugh suggests that "the Septuagint translators coined this word to describe the activity of Sabbath keeping."[19]

Why did the writer of Hebrews choose this particular word? Joseph A. Pipa maintains that he chose this term

> as a play on words. He emphasizes that the spiritual, eternal rest promised by God has not been fulfilled; the promise of eternal rest remains, and they must enter it by persevering faith. That is, one enters this

spiritual rest by faith in the Lord Jesus Christ, but it will be fully realized only when one enters the eternal rest of glory. Thus, he emphasizes the ongoing need to persevere.

. . . He selects or coins *sabbatismos* because, in addition to referring to spiritual rest, it suggests as well an observance of that rest by a "Sabbath-keeping." Because the promised rest lies ahead for the New Covenant people, they are to strive to enter the future rest. Yet as they do so, they anticipate it by continuing to keep the Sabbath.[20]

Arthur W. Pink adds,

Here then is a plain, positive, unequivocal declaration by the Spirit of God. "There remaineth therefore a Sabbath-keeping." Nothing could be simpler, nothing less ambiguous. The striking thing is that this statement occurs in the very epistle whose theme is the superiority of *Christianity* over Judaism; written to those addressed as "holy brethren, partakers of the heavenly calling." Therefore, it cannot be gainsaid that Hebrews 4:9 refers directly to the *Christian Sabbath.* Hence we solemnly and emphatically declare that any man who says there is no Christian Sabbath takes direct issue with the *New Testament* Scriptures.[21]

The resurrection rest, which we celebrate on the first day of the week, is not the end or the fulfillment: it is the beginning. It is the beginning of life eternal, of the abundant and blessed rest in Jesus. Sunday is a type of, and testimony to, the saints' experience in heaven.

It is also a witness against hell. Those who will not rest in Jesus will be judged by Jesus, and they will never rest. Christ's resurrection, a sign to us of blessing and hope, is as well a sign of certain judgment to the world. God "has set a day when he will judge the world with justice by the man he has appointed. He has given proof of this to all men by raising him from the dead" (Acts 17:31).

The Sabbath is still appointed for all men everywhere. Those who reject it must still die spiritually. The first day of every week silently, but pointedly, invites all the inhabitants of the earth to rest in Jesus. God "now . . . commands all people everywhere to repent" (Acts 17:30). Every day some do, but many others do not. Let us see to it that not one of us hardens his or her heart and falls short of entering God's rest.

The Heidelberg Catechism asks, "What does God require in the fourth commandment?" The answer is,

> First, that the ministry of the gospel and the schools be maintained, and that I, especially on the Sabbath, that is, the day of rest, diligently attend the church of God, to learn God's word, to use the sacraments, to call publicly upon the Lord, and to give Christian alms. Second, that all the days of my life I rest from my evil works, let the Lord work in me by His Holy Spirit, and thus begin in this life the eternal Sabbath.

Thus, as Pipa argues, "The theology of accomplished redemption does not annul a continued Sabbath-keeping, but requires it."[22]

REVIEW

1. How is the relationship between the Sabbath and the Lord's Day like the relationship between an acorn and an oak?

2. How does Jesus' resurrection from the dead advance and improve our understanding of the Sabbath?

3. How are the Old and New Covenants related? What two characteristics need to be kept in mind?

4. Who is the central figure who provides continuity between the covenants?

5. Who is the Lord of the Sabbath? When did he *become* Lord of the Sabbath?

6. What is the essential meaning of the Sabbath?

7. Why do New Covenant believers celebrate the Sabbath on the first day of the week? What is the theological reason for doing so? What is the historical argument for the change of day?

8. What is the significance of Pentecost? What is the relationship of Pentecost to the Sabbath as a celebration of redemption? What day of the week was Pentecost?

9. What other biblical evidence calls attention to the importance of Sunday as a new day for celebration?

10. What is the Final Sabbath?

11. Is the possession of eternal rest certain for all who profess faith? What is the significance of the Spirit's warnings in Hebrews 4?

12. How does God prepare us to enter and enjoy his Final Sabbath?

13. What does being faithful require of us?

14. Does the resurrection of Jesus mean that we no longer have to keep any Sabbath?

15. Does the Sabbath have any message for unbelievers?

RESPONSE

1. The essential unity of the Sabbath and the Lord's Day reflects the essential unity of the Old and New Testaments. Am I a thoroughly biblical Christian, or have I largely dismissed Old Testament revelation?

2. Jesus identifies himself as God by applying to himself Old Testament texts that refer to the LORD. When I read the Old Testament, do I recognize Christ revealed in its pages? Why or why not?

3. If the message of the Sabbath has always been that true rest can only be found in Christ, then how were people saved before Christ came (see Romans 4:1–13)? How have people been saved since Christ came?

4. How important was the doctrine of the resurrection of Jesus from the dead to the writers of the New Testament? How important is it in many churches today? How important is it in *my* church? To *me*? Why?

5. How is Pentecost a great encouragement to evangelism and missions?

6. How does participation in the Lord's Supper remind me of the Final Sabbath that is still to come?

7. Does everyone who *professes* faith necessarily *possess* it? May I have assurance that I believe? How? What will happen to those who do not persevere in faith?

8. When I meet with others for worship, am I an active encourager (Hebrews 10:25) or merely a spectator? What do I need to do that I am not doing?

9. Do I read the book of Revelation to find encouragement and hope? Why or why not? If the book frightens me, do I really understand its purpose?

10. Am I ready to enjoy Sunday as a taste of heaven? What will I do for my family, friends, and neighbors who are not ready?

FIVE

SABBATH WARS:
THE CONFLICT BEGUN

I used to go with the multitude,
leading the procession to the house of God,
with shouts of joy and thanksgiving
among the festive throng.
—*Psalm 42:4*

This is the day the Lord hath made;
He calls the hours his own;
Let heav'n rejoice, let earth be glad,
And praise surround the throne.
—*Isaac Watts, 1719*

Jesus was accused by the Pharisees of violating the fourth commandment on no fewer than six different occasions in the gospel records. Indeed, he had no sooner begun his public ministry by teaching in the synagogue at Nazareth on a Sabbath than the Jews were filled with rage and wanted to throw him off a cliff (Luke 4:16–30)! Does it seem strange to you that the symbol of holy rest and peace should be the occasion for such angry and violent conflict? It should not surprise us, for ever since the Fall, the Sabbath has been a day of unholy unrest and controversy.

In this chapter we want to consider the intention of the Sabbath as it was originally given, and then its captivity and corruption by religious but legalistic people.

The Intention of the Sabbath

A. W. Pink rightly notes that the Sabbath was "designed as a day of gladness and not of gloom."[1] It was intended by its Creator to be a day of rest and worship in celebration of God's wonderful works. The Sabbath promised both physical and spiritual refreshment for the whole person.

For six days people were to labor and complete all their work. But the seventh day was to be a Sabbath. The word *sabbath* literally means "rest." God commanded,

> On it you shall not do any work, neither you, nor your son or daughter, nor your manservant or maidservant, nor your animals, nor the alien within your gates. (Exodus 20:10)

The Sabbath was a day off from work, a day when men and women, their families and servants, visitors, and even livestock could enjoy the gift of rest from God.

It was a day for "complete rest" (Exodus 35:2 NASB), a day to leave the briefcase at the office and the tools locked up in the shed. Even during the busy times of the year, during the plowing season and harvest, the people were commanded to rest on the seventh day in honor of, and obedience to, the Lord who made heaven and earth (Exodus 34:21; 35:1–3).

Moonlighting was prohibited on the Sabbath. The worker who tried to get ahead of others by working on the Sabbath day was subject to the death penalty. As Dawn observes,

> A major blessing of Sabbath keeping is that it forces us to rely on God for our future. On that day we do nothing to create our own way. We abstain from work, from our incessant need to produce and accomplish, from all the anxieties about how we can be successful in all that we have to do to get ahead. The result is that we can let God be God in our lives.[2]

Once, while the Israelites were in the wilderness, they found a man gathering wood on the Sabbath. He did not want any rest from his labors. He was even willing to break the law of God if that would enable him to get ahead of his neighbors. Those who discovered the man detained him and kept him in custody because it was not clear to them what should be done with him. Then the Lord said to Moses, "The man must die" (Numbers 15:32–36). The whole assembly took the offender outside the camp and put him to death in a community affirmation of the Sabbath and condemnation of lawlessness.

It is one thing to sin unintentionally out of ignorance or weakness, but it is quite another to sin knowingly and defiantly.

> Anyone who sins defiantly, whether native-born or alien, blasphemes the LORD, and that person must be cut off from his people. Because he has despised the LORD's word and broken his commands, that person must surely be cut off; his guilt remains on him. (Numbers 15:30–31)

The death penalty was added to the fourth commandment in Israel in order to guarantee rest. It was not left for individuals to decide whether they wanted rest or not. God commanded the seventh day to be a Sabbath of complete rest to the Lord. Israel was a nation in covenant with God, and men like the moonlighting wood-gatherer who defiantly broke his commandments were covenant-breakers and traitors. They were to be cut off from among the people.

What does it mean to rest? Rest clearly means cessation from work, but it also means more.

> Six days do your work, but on the seventh day do not work, so that your ox and your donkey may rest and the slave born in your household, and the alien as well, may be refreshed. (Exodus 23:12)

Rest is here defined as refreshment. The fact that we are not working does not necessarily mean that we are resting:

rest means refreshment. The word translated "refresh" in the Old Testament also means "breathe." A man is refreshed when, having exhausted himself, he recovers his breath. The Sabbath, therefore, is a God-given opportunity to catch our breath in the midst of our weekly routine of work. It is intended to be a break, an opportunity to pause and be refreshed, to catch our breath before going back to work.

Old Testament believers received the Sabbath as a day of welcome relief and restoration because it provided the opportunity for much-needed physical rest and refreshment. They were to remember that they had lived bitter lives as slaves under ruthless Egyptian taskmasters, and that God had given them relief (Deuteronomy 5:15; Exodus 1:11–14). Truly the Sabbath was appointed to be a blessing.

But the Sabbath was appointed to minister to the whole person, and it was therefore also a day of spiritual rest. It was to be a "complete rest to the LORD" (Exodus 35:2 NASB). The Sabbath keeps us from playing God. It calls us to cease from our works and to rest in, and enjoy the fruit of, his works. The world, after all, does not depend upon our efforts to keep it going. We can all take a day off, and the world will still be here in the morning, because God upholds it by the word of his power. We live and move and have our being in him (Acts 17:28). "We always try to be in control of our lives, but the seventh-day observance reminds us that God is the master of time."[3] This is God's world, not ours, and keeping his Sabbath signals our acceptance of his right to rule over us.

The Sabbath in the Old Covenant was a picture of salvation by the sovereign grace of God. As it commemorated God's great act of deliverance in the Old Testament, the Exodus, the Sabbath reminded people that it was not by their works that they could be delivered, but by his power. " 'Not by might nor by power, but by my Spirit,' says the LORD Almighty" (Zechariah 4:6).

This declaration of sovereign grace anticipated the coming of the promised Deliverer. As the Sabbath looked forward to the salvation to be revealed one day in Christ Jesus, it taught people that they could obtain rest only by ceasing from their own efforts and trusting fully in the work of the Redeemer. Redemption is not of man; it is all of God. "Salvation comes from the LORD" (Jonah 2:9).

The Sabbath in the Old Testament, then, was a day for physical and spiritual refreshment and joyful celebration of creation and redemption. It was a holiday providing opportunity for both physical rest and spiritual worship. No wonder the psalmist led the procession to the house of God with shouts of joy and thanksgiving (Psalm 42:4)! The Sabbath was a festive occasion.

THE BABYLONIAN CAPTIVITY OF THE SABBATH

This wonderful holiday that was given by God was soon defiled and perverted by ungodly humanity. The natural (that is, unregenerate) man does not want to rest in God's completed works, but in his own. The natural man is at war with God and battles all his commandments. Sabbath wars are only part of a much larger rebellion against the authority of God in all of life. Paul writes,

> Those who live according to the sinful nature have their minds set on what that nature desires; but those who live in accordance with the Spirit have their

minds set on what the Spirit desires. The mind of sinful man is death, but the mind controlled by the Spirit is life and peace; the sinful mind is hostile to God. It does not submit to God's law, nor can it do so. Those controlled by the sinful nature cannot please God. (Romans 8:5–8; see also Psalm 2:1–3)

Fallen man, wanting to be his own god and redeemer, came to see the Sabbath as an interruption of his own saving work. Instead of seeing the Sabbath as a blessing that God gave to him, he resented it as one day in seven that God took away from him.

Consequently, the Sabbath has historically been abused, neglected, and ignored. In Israel and Judah, neglect of the Sabbath (among other things) brought judgment and captivity at the hands of the Assyrians and Babylonians. The Assyrians scattered captive populations among the nations, making certain that there were not enough people of any one nationality living near each other to cause any problems. Saggs observes, "The number of people affected by Assyrian deportations was enormous; it has been estimated that in the final three centuries of the Assyrian empire it amounted to between four and five million."[4]

The Babylonians, however, brought the best and most promising of each conquered nation to their own country to be reeducated in accordance with their religious, philosophical, and political ideals. That period in Israel's experience was called the Babylonian Captivity or the Exile, because the people were put out of the land by God so that it could obtain the rest that they had denied it (2 Chronicles 36:15–21).

As they were resettled in other countries, the Jews

rubbed shoulders with cultures that were even more degenerate than their own. Not only were the people captives, but so were their customs and practices, including the Sabbath.

The Babylonians, for example, observed the seventh, fourteenth, twenty-first, and twenty-eighth days of certain months as special days to be spent in penance and prayer. They didn't eat, put on clean clothes, travel, or even dress a wound. And they didn't work.

But the Babylonian *shappatu* was not a day of rest and celebration. It was a day of bad luck. S. Moscati notes, "The daily life of the Babylonians and Assyrians was perpetually overshadowed by the fear of demons."[5] They kept a kind of Sabbath not because they respected God's law, but because they feared Murphy's Law.[6] They were afraid that if they did anything, it was bound to backfire on them.

The king could not travel by chariot, for fear that if he did, he would almost certainly fall off and be injured or killed. They were concerned that if a woman baked bread, she might burn the house down. If a builder went to his job, he would probably drop a brick on his toe. Something bad was bound to happen. Like the Hebrew Sabbath, the Babylonian *shappatu* was a day off from work, but it was definitely not a day for joyful celebration.

It was during this period, when the Jews were dominated by the Assyrians and the Babylonians, that the place and nature of the law became twisted in their thinking. We tend to underestimate the influence of these peoples on the spiritual life of Israel, but as Israeli author Baruch Maoz reminds us,

> The Babylonians, followed by the Medes and the Persians, were less coercive [than the Assyrians] but

their apparent meekness was misleading and Israel was to a very large extent transformed by it: the Babylonian calendar was adopted and "Wise Men" replaced the priests and the Israelite political authorities. Contrary to what the rabbis would have us believe, Judaism is a hybrid religion: the Israel that came out of Babylon was very different from the nation which originally went into exile there.[7]

"The just shall live by faith" is an Old Testament saying (Habakkuk 2:4), but many Jews began to believe that they could save themselves by keeping God's law. After all, they reasoned, they lived in exile because they had broken the law. Now if they only kept the law, they could save themselves. They didn't need God's grace. They just needed to work very hard to do what God said. Then they would be good enough to deserve God's blessings.

The effects of that kind of thinking upon the Sabbath were tragic. Keeping the Sabbath became one of the works that people must do in order to be saved. Therefore, the elders and rabbis became very interested in spelling out precisely what people could and could not do on the Sabbath. The spirit and intention of the law became lost in a sea of technicalities.

This was the origin of what we earlier called the casuistic approach to the Sabbath. The conclusions of the elders and rabbis formed a body of oral traditions that later were collected in the Talmud. The Talmud is the written form of the oral traditions that grew out of the Exile, when the sons of Israel were influenced by their superstitious neighbors.

The tractate entitled *Shabbath* in the Talmud lists thirty-nine categories of work that are prohibited on the Sabbath. Each one of these categories is further subdivided into thirty-nine sections, making over 1,500 rules and regulations that one who would be righteous must keep. Can you imagine the burden of trying to memorize and keep 1,500 rules and regulations that apply to just this one day? On this twisted and distorted Sabbath it was forbidden to unfasten a button, cut your toenails, or carry anything heavier than a dried fig. A man could not wear false teeth, because if they fell out, he would have to carry them, and that would be work. A tailor could not carry a needle in his pocket on the Sabbath because that was one of the tools of his trade, so carrying it would be work.

The rabbis themselves admitted that all these rules and regulations were like a mountain hanging by a thread, but they justified what they did because they said the rules in Scripture were so brief. Scripture does not adequately define what constitutes work, they said, and so they assumed the responsibility to tell the people what was work and make sure that they didn't do any. This gave birth to a nation of spies. People were continually looking for someone who was doing something forbidden.

Thus, the day that God had appointed as a day of rest, celebration, worship, joy, and physical and spiritual refreshment was turned into a restrictive, confining, oppressive, and gloomy day. The festival had turned into a funeral. Dancing had become mourning.[8]

This was the Sabbath observance confronted by the Lord of glory when the Word became flesh and dwelt among us. It had the appearance of being biblical, but at heart it was Babylonian. The Pharisees, drawing from the tradition of the elders, had effectively subverted God's gift of grace and taken it captive to their own legalistic and self-saving intentions.

REVIEW

1. Was the Sabbath designed to be a day of gladness or of gloom?
2. What does the word *sabbath* mean? What kind of rest is it?
3. What happened to the man who gathered wood on the Sabbath? Why?
4. Is there a biblical distinction between unintentional and defiant sins?
5. Is the biblical meaning of rest satisfied by physical inactivity? What more is meant?
6. What was the historical experience of the Jews that they were to remember each Sabbath day?
7. What is spiritual rest?
8. What is the relationship between the Sabbath and the sovereignty of God?
9. How was the Sabbath a picture of redemption in the Old Testament?
10. What did the great redemptive act of the Old Testament, the Exodus, anticipate or look forward to?
11. Was the Sabbath of the Old Testament kept as a happy holiday, or was it a mournful memorial?
12. When did people begin to abuse and neglect God's Sabbath?
13. Why do people neglect the Sabbath?

14. What did neglect of the Sabbath (among other sins) bring to the northern kingdom of Israel? And to the southern kingdom of Judah?

15. What was the Babylonian *shappatu*? How was it like the Sabbath? How was it different?

16. What influence did the Assyrians and Babylonians have on the Jewish understanding and keeping of the Sabbath?

17. What is the Talmud, and how did it come to be written?

18. How did the rabbis justify making so many rules and regulations to govern Sabbath activities?

19. What were the effects of this casuistic approach to the Sabbath?

20. What is legalism, and how were the Pharisees legalistic?

RESPONSE

1. Jesus was the divine Lawgiver. Do I also think of him in his human nature as a law-keeper? If I am to be like him, what does that mean for me with respect to the Sabbath?

2. In my experience, has the Sabbath been a day of gladness or a day of gloom? Why?

3. Do I need a day of "complete rest" to catch my breath physically, spiritually, and emotionally? What things in my life suggest that I do?

4. "Sin is lawlessness" (1 John 3:4). I commit some sins out of ignorance, because I don't know any better. What sins am I committing knowingly and defiantly?

5. How does keeping the Sabbath day holy signal my acceptance of God's sovereignty?

6. Do I think of the Sabbath as a gift of grace or as twenty-four hours that God has taken away from me?

7. There is a little bit of the legalist in every one of us. How does legalism express itself in my life? In my attitude toward the Sabbath?

8. Is the Lord's Day in my life a festival or a funeral? What should it be? If my attitude toward the Sabbath is wrong, how can I begin to change it?

SIX

SABBATH WARS:
THE BATTLE WON

The Son of Man is Lord
even of the Sabbath.
—*Mark 2:28*

May thy gospel's joyful sound
Conquer sinners, comfort saints;
May the fruits of grace abound,
Bring relief for all complaints:
Thus may all our Sabbaths prove,
Till we join the church above,
Thus may all our Sabbaths prove,
Till we join the church above.
—*John Newton, 1774*

Calvin traced the origin of the term *Pharisee* to a word meaning "to explain" or "to expound."[1] The Pharisees saw themselves as the skilled interpreters and faithful protectors of God's law. Scholars believe that the Pharisees developed as a sect or party during the period prior to the Maccabean War—as a conservative reaction to the compromising spirit of some who were adopting Greek customs.

While they may have meant well in the beginning, by Jesus' day the Pharisees were notable for their legalism, hypocrisy, self-righteousness, and spiritual pride. In attempting to protect God's law, they actually undermined its authority by burying it beneath layers of rabbinic traditions. In their minds, the traditions of the elders became equally authoritative with the Word of God, and they were no longer able to distinguish between the two.

On one occasion, when the Pharisees criticized Jesus' disciples for not carefully observing their traditions, Jesus characteristically cut right to the heart of the issue. He said,

> "You have let go of the commands of God and are holding on to the traditions of men."
> And he said to them: "You have a fine way of setting aside the commands of God in order to observe your own traditions!" (Mark 7:8–9)

The Pharisees had failed to protect the law of God and were guilty of actually setting aside God's commands in favor of their own. The Pharisaic Sabbath of Jesus' day suffered in the same way. It was the opposite of the day of joyful celebration that God had blessed and sanctified for mankind. In trying to interpret what it meant to work on the Sabbath, the rabbinic fathers had overlaid God's law with more than 1,500 rules and regulations. The people may have returned to the land, but the Sabbath was still in captivity.

THE LIBERATION OF THE SABBATH

When God the eternal Son took upon himself the nature of a man and visited his people, he came to set the captives free, including the captive Sabbath. Jesus challenged the Pharisaic distortions of his holy day. He repeatedly and purposely did things on the Sabbath that violated their legalistic understanding of Sabbath keeping.

Jesus came to restore the law, including the fourth commandment, not to dismantle it (see Matthew 5:17–20). As J. C. Ryle notes, Christ "no more abolishes the Sabbath, than a man destroys a house when he cleans off the moss or weeds from its roof."[2] Richard Cecil agrees that "Christ came not to abolish the Sabbath, . . . but to explain and enforce it."[3]

Jesus blasted the Pharisaic Sabbath, but in doing so he did not harm the biblical Sabbath at all. Indeed, he liberated it, restored it, and filled it full of meaning once again (Matthew 5:17).[4] Just as Jesus cleansed the temple of its money changers and merchants by overturning their tables and forcefully driving them away, so he also delivered the Sabbath of its rabbinic legalism by walking directly into the camp of his enemies and disarming them by his definitive works of mercy.

THE LORD OF THE SABBATH

How did Jesus challenge the Pharisaic Sabbath and free the day to fulfill its original intention? When did his enemies accuse him of violating the fourth commandment? What were the skirmishes and battles the Son of Man fought and won to secure victory for his people in the Sabbath wars?

1. The Battle of the Wheat Field (Mark 2:23–28)[5]

Jesus and his disciples were passing through the grainfields one Sabbath. The disciples were hungry, and as they walked among the stalks of wheat, they were picking the heads of grain, grinding them in their fingers, and putting them into their mouths.

Some of the Pharisees saw them and complained to Jesus that his disciples were breaking the Sabbath. From their point of view, his disciples were working. More specifically, they were (1) harvesting, as they picked the heads of grain, (2) threshing, as they separated the grain from the stalk, (3) winnowing, as they blew away the chaff, and (4) milling, as they ground the grain between their fingers.

All of these things were forbidden by the tradition of the elders, as reflected in the Talmud. But were they violating the Scriptures? God's law allowed them to pass through their neighbor's vineyard or standing grain and eat until they were satisfied, but they could not take more than they required (Deuteronomy 23:24–25). All that they did was lawful, but was it lawful on the Sabbath?

Jesus defended his disciples, as he defended himself against the Evil One in the wilderness, by appealing to the Word of God: When David was hungry and in need while fleeing from Saul, he and his companions properly ate the consecrated bread that was supposed to be eaten only by the priests (1 Samuel 21:1–6).

God did not condemn David for eating the consecrated bread, and neither did the Pharisees. David was God's servant doing God's business, however imperfectly, and he received God's provision for his needs, including hunger.

Wielding that great sword of the Word, Jesus went on to insist that the Sabbath was made for man, and not the other way around. God delights in mercy more than in sacrifice, and in substance more than in ceremony (see Matthew 12:7).

As Williamson observes, "The disciples kept the sabbath in a different way than the Pharisees because they served Christ."[6] The actions of the disciples may have tweaked the self-righteous consciences of the Pharisees, but they did not violate the will of him who is Lord of the Sabbath. Works of necessity, such as eating, do not violate the intent of the rest that God has provided.

In this first Sabbath engagement, Jesus put his enemies to flight and boldly asserted that he alone had authority over the Sabbath. In making this claim, no one could fail to see that Jesus was affirming his own identity as God—the very same God who blessed the Sabbath day and made it holy when he rested from his work of creating (Genesis 2:3). Anyone today who wants to debate whether or not the Lord's Day is legitimately called the Christian Sabbath will have to argue with Jesus, the Lord of the Sabbath.

2. The Shriveled-Hand Skirmish (Mark 3:1–6)[7]

On another Sabbath, Jesus went into a synagogue and there encountered a man who had a shriveled hand. The Pharisees were watching him closely to see if he would heal the man, so that they could pounce on him for "working" on the Sabbath. This behavior is typical of Pharisees, both ancient and modern. They don't want to celebrate; they only want to criticize. Still smarting from their earlier defeat, they were looking for an opportunity to even the score.

Unlike the previous confrontation, which occurred outside in the fields, this clash took place inside a synagogue, where people had gathered to worship God.

Knowing the tactics of his opponents, Jesus had the disabled man stand up in front of everyone. There was no question about the propriety of worshiping on the Sabbath, but what about healing? Looking intently at the Pharisees, Jesus asked them, "Which is lawful on the Sabbath: to do good or to do evil, to save life or to kill?"

If Jesus counterattacked in the wheat field, here he launched a stunning preemptive strike. Before the Pharisees could attack him, Jesus launched his own assault from an unexpected direction. Catching them by surprise before they could set their trap, his words struck them like so many bullets raking their ranks with deadly accuracy.

Defensive and disarmed, how could they respond? Since it is never lawful to do evil or to kill, they would have to reply, "to do good and to save life." But if they said that, they would have to approve of Jesus healing the man in front of them. How could they publicly say what they privately thought, that it was actually better to look the other way than to help?

Burning with anger[8] and deeply distressed by the stubbornness of their hearts, Jesus then healed the man so that his useless hand was immediately and completely restored.

His act of healing was not a violation of the Sabbath as God gave it. Works of mercy and compassion are consistent with the rest and redemption that God graciously provides. But healing the disabled man *was* a violation of the Sabbath traditions that had grown out of the Exile. According to the rabbis, it was forbidden even to put a bandage on a cut.

With his haunting question still ringing in their ears, "Which is lawful on the Sabbath: to do good or to do evil, to save life or to kill?" the Pharisees began to plot with the Herodians[9] how to kill Jesus. In their minds, it was preferable to murder Jesus rather than to allow him to continue to bless and heal people on the Sabbath!

3. The Crippled-Woman Conflict (Luke 13:10–17)

Jesus crossed spiritual swords with a religious leader one Sabbath when he was teaching in a synagogue. There was a woman worshiping there who had been ill for eighteen years. For almost two decades this poor woman had been doubled up in pain, unable to straighten up at all. It is a remarkable commentary on her spiritual commitment that she was there at all. Many people today permit far less to keep them from the assembly of the saints.

When our Lord saw her, he called her forward and freed her from her sickness. Immediately she was able to straighten up and stand normally again. What a marvelous sight to see!

But instead of being grateful, the synagogue official became indignant, annoyed that Jesus had done such a thing on the Sabbath. He began to lash out at the crowd, saying, "There are six days for work. So come and be healed on those days, not on the Sabbath."

Instead of rejoicing in the power of God displayed in the deliverance of this woman, a faithful member of his flock, this so-called shepherd of Israel was angry with Jesus for violating a tradition of the elders.

Jesus responded by calling him what he was, a hypocrite. In the eyes of the Pharisees, it was okay to lead a thirsty donkey to water, but it was morally wrong to free a sick woman from chronic disease and pain on the Sabbath. They were hypocrites.

All of Jesus' opponents were humiliated, but the common people rejoiced because of what they had seen. Jesus had turned a sour Sabbath into a holy celebration of God and his works.

4. The Dropsy Disaster (Luke 14:1–6)

After a synagogue service, people in Jesus' day often did what people do today after Sunday morning worship: they went home and had dinner. The Sabbath dinner was often the best meal of the week, and guests were frequently invited to share the blessing. One Sabbath, Jesus was invited into the home of a prominent Pharisee to eat. Although the offer of hospitality is normally an invitation to relax and be refreshed, Luke tells us that again they were watching Jesus closely, hoping to catch him in some Sabbath violation.

One of the guests was a man who was suffering from dropsy. The Greek word for dropsy is a medical term that we still use today, *edema*. Edema is swelling caused by the retention of too much fluid in body cavities and tissues. It may be local, as when you sprain your knee and it swells, or it may be general. Dropsy is a general edema, usually caused by heart or kidney disease. It can be quite uncomfortable, and, if left unattended, can even be fatal.

The unhealthy guest was not there by chance. This poor, sick man was the bait in a trap set by the Pharisees, and Jesus was the intended prey.

Jesus never hesitated, even for a moment. Seizing the initiative, he asked the spiritual experts, the lawyers, "Is it lawful to heal on the Sabbath or not?"

Is it lawful? Jesus made his appeal not to the obvious need of the visibly suffering man, or to humanitarian concerns, but to the intent of the Lawgiver. The distinction is important. Our actions must be governed not by what feels right, but by what is right—not by our emotions, but by the Word of God. As in other confrontations, his opponents would not answer him.

Demonstrating the correct response, rather than merely verbalizing it, Jesus healed the man in front of them all. Then he asked them whether, if they had a son or an ox that fell into a well on the Sabbath, they would immediately pull him out. Obviously, they would. And if it was proper to show that kind of concern for the needs of animals, then why would anyone question the propriety of delivering this man from his suffering?

The trappers were trapped. Again there was nothing that they had the strength, ability, or courage to say. The Lord of the Sabbath turned their evil plan for him into a strategic disaster for themselves.

5. The Battle of Bethesda (John 5:1–9)

Once when Jesus went up to Jerusalem to celebrate a feast, he came to a pool called Bethesda, which was near the Sheep Gate. There were many disabled people near the pool, including one man who had been unable to walk for thirty-eight years. He was lying by the pool, hoping to be the first one into the water when an angel of the Lord stirred it up, so that he could be made well. But he didn't have the strength to get into the water fast enough by himself, and he didn't have anyone to help him.

When Jesus saw him and learned that he had been in this condition for a long time, he asked the invalid, "Do you want to get well?" Hoping that Jesus would just help him get into the water before the others, the man replied affirmatively. Jesus told him to pick up the mat he had been lying on and walk. Immediately the man was cured and did as Jesus told him. John adds, "The day on which this took place was a Sabbath" (v. 9).

As the man was walking away, the Jews stopped him and accused him of breaking the law by carrying his mat. That bed was certainly heavier than a dried fig, and he was therefore a Sabbath-breaker. They could not rejoice with him in his newfound steps, and they would not glorify God for his mighty works. All they could see was him carrying that mat, and they were annoyed.

They asked him who had authorized him to pick up his

mat and walk, but the man did not know the name of the one who had healed him. It was the Lord of the Sabbath who had made him well on his holy day.

John adds that "because Jesus was doing these things on the Sabbath, the Jews persecuted him." Jesus, however, defended his Sabbath works as imitative of God's works, saying, "My Father is always at his work to this very day, and I, too, am working" (vv. 16–17). It is right for us, as well, to imitate our Father by doing good on the Lord's Day.

6. The Spit Spat (John 9:1–41)

John records that Jesus healed a man who had been blind since birth. His disciples saw the blind man and wanted to know who was responsible for his condition. Someone must have done something wrong. Had he sinned, or were his parents to blame?

Jesus replied that neither the man nor his parents were to blame for his blindness, "but this happened so that the work of God might be displayed in his life" (v. 3). While suffering is in general a consequence of sin, suffering is not always a direct consequence of any particular sin. This man's suffering was to provide the opportunity for Jesus to reveal himself to his disciples as "the light of the world" (v. 5).

Jesus spat on the ground, made mud with the saliva, applied the mud to the blind man's eyes, and told him to go and wash in the Pool of Siloam. The blind man did that, and, to everyone's amazement, he went home seeing.

All of his neighbors and those who had seen the man

begging were astonished by what had happened. Some questioned whether he was actually the same man they had known. They brought him to the Pharisees. Again John adds, "Now the day on which Jesus had made the mud and opened the man's eyes was a Sabbath" (v. 14).

This miracle was a tremendous testimony to the reality of Jesus' claim to be the Messiah. Deliverance, freedom, and healing had come (Isaiah 42:1–7)! But the Pharisees could not see that. All they could see was Jesus mixing the mud with his fingers and healing on the Sabbath. Such "work" was forbidden by the regulations of the rabbis.

Some of the Pharisees concluded, "This man is not from God, for he does not keep the Sabbath" (John 9:16). But others asked how a sinner could perform such miracles.

The Pharisees pressed their investigation with inquisitorial finesse, working first on the formerly blind man and then on his parents, trying in vain to discredit the miracle that had taken place. Despite their best threats, they could not get either the man or his parents to change their story. Finally, in desperation, they hurled insults at the man. His steady reply stymied them, and they could do nothing more than throw him out (vv. 17–34).[10]

Once more, Jesus met his enemies and soundly defeated them on what they had falsely believed was their own spiritual ground. Jesus took the field. His enemies could not overcome him. The Pharisees were no match legally, spiritually, or theologically for Immanuel. The Son of Man judges all men. The man who had been physically blind since birth could now see. The self-righteous Pharisees, who claimed they could see, were spiritually blind (vv. 35–41).

THE CONFLICT RESOLVED

Thus there was conflict between Jesus and the Pharisees over the Sabbath. Jesus at times seemed to go out of his way to call attention to the conflict. He didn't need to make mud in order to heal the blind man. He only needed to speak and the man would be healed. But he wanted people to *see* as well as hear that he was Lord of the Sabbath.

The day of rest had become an unbelievable day of bondage, with people laboring under a burden of oppressive traditions. Liberty had become slavery, rejoicing had become spying, and Jesus could not do godly things on the Sabbath without being criticized and condemned in the name of so-called righteousness.

The conflict was not so much a personal matter between Jesus and the Pharisees as it was a conflict between the holy Sabbath of God and the painfully distorted Pharisaic Sabbath. It was part of Jesus' mission to liberate, heal, and redeem the Sabbath from captivity.

Significantly, most of these six clashes had to do with healing, and all of them had to do with the body. It was Jesus' custom on the Sabbath day to go into the synagogues to teach and participate in the reading of the Word and prayer. The Pharisees had no conflict with him regarding worship on the Sabbath. Their controversy centered on their understanding of rest and refreshment.

Jesus taught both by precept and by example that it is proper to do those things on the Sabbath which refresh, heal, and restore breath and strength to the body. Thus, not only works of worship and piety, but also works of necessity and mercy, are appropriate Sabbath activities.[11]

The resolution of Sabbath conflicts lies in understanding who Jesus is and submitting to him. Sabbath battles cease only when in Christ our hearts have peace.

Early in his ministry, Jesus insisted, "The Sabbath was made for man, not man for the Sabbath" (Mark 2:27). The Sabbath was appointed by God to meet the needs of man as a day of rest, refreshment, and enjoyment. It was intended by God to be the best day of the week—the day that people would look and long for, and be glad to enjoy.

In this series of conflicts, Jesus in effect was saying, "Look, you Pharisees—look at what you've done with my day. I gave it to make you holy, healthy, and happy, and instead you have used it to oppress people and enslave their consciences to man-made rules and regulations that I never commanded. You've forgotten that first I made man, and then I made the Sabbath."

The Pharisees accused Jesus of violating the Sabbath, and he accused them of not even knowing what the Sabbath was all about.

The real Sabbath conflicts are not over Sabbath activities *per se,* but over the authority of Christ. Jesus insisted, "The Son of Man is Lord even of the Sabbath" (Mark 2:28). Here is the real issue: is Jesus Christ *Lord,* or is he not? If he is, then he is Lord of the Sabbath and has the authority to define its intention, function, meaning, and proper use. Ryle declares,

> Our Lord claims the right to dispense with all the traditional rules, and man-made laws about the Sabbath, with which the Pharisees had overloaded the day of rest. As Son of man, who came not to destroy,

but to save, He asserts His power to set free the blessed Sabbath from the false and superstitious notions with which the Rabbins had clogged and poisoned it, and to restore it to its proper meaning and use. He declares that the Sabbath is His day,—His by creation and institution, since He first gave it in Paradise and at Sinai,—and proclaims His determination to defend and purify His day from Jewish imposition, and to give it to His disciples as a day of blessing, comfort, and benefit, according to its original intention.[12]

To charge him with violating the Sabbath that he had ordained, as the Pharisees charged him, was a denial of his proper authority as Lord.

The Sabbath was and is *his day,* appointed by him for men and women to honor him as Creator and Redeemer, the One in whom we find and obtain physical and spiritual rest. This is the essential meaning of the Sabbath or Lord's Day.

The Jews rejected the Sabbath rest because they rejected Christ as Lord. So it is today. Men reject the Lord's Day rest because they reject the Lord of the day.

The Sabbath is a principle of life. God demanded that people rest, and if they rejected the rest that God provided, they were to be put to death. The rejection of the Sabbath rest today still carries a death penalty, though not by civil authorities.[13] Those who reject God's rest and insist on their full ability to labor without ceasing bring death upon themselves in the form of unrelieved stress, hypertension, heart attacks, strokes, and a multitude of diseases. Sabbath breaking still brings death physically.

And it brings death spiritually. The teaching of the Sabbath is that we cannot save ourselves by any or even all of our works. It is only when we cease from our works and rest in the full and finished work of Jesus Christ alone that we obtain final rest. Men who reject the work of Christ in favor of their own works will all die the second death. And, as R. M. M'Cheyne notes, "There are no Sabbaths in hell."[14]

There is no rest, no Sabbath, for the wicked.

REVIEW

1. Who were the Pharisees, and what were they noted for in Jesus' day?
2. How did they attempt to preserve and protect God's law? Did they succeed in their efforts?
3. Did Jesus agree with the Pharisaic understanding of God's law?
4. How did Jesus demonstrate his response to the Pharisaic observance of the Sabbath?
5. What was the issue in "the Battle of the Wheat Field?" Who won? How?
6. Is it lawful to do works of necessity on the Sabbath? How do you know?
7. What was "the Shriveled-Hand Skirmish?" Who won? How?
8. Did Jesus break his own law by healing on the Sabbath? What did he violate that so angered the Pharisees that they conspired to kill him?
9. Is it lawful to do works of mercy and kindness on the Sabbath? How do you know?

10. What was the issue in "the Crippled-Woman Conflict?" Who won? How?

11. What is dropsy? Why was a man with this disease invited to the Pharisee's home on the Sabbath? What did Jesus do?

12. What key question did Jesus ask before healing the man with dropsy? What must govern all of our actions?

13. What happened when Jesus went to the pool called Bethesda? Why were the Jews displeased to see this man carrying the mat he had been lying on?

14. Who was to blame for the blindness of the man who had been blind since birth?

15. How did this miracle show that Jesus was the Messiah? What did the Pharisees conclude about him? Why?

16. What did Jesus conclude about the Pharisees? Why?

17. What categories of activities are appropriate to do on the Sabbath?

18. What is the key to resolving Sabbath wars or conflicts? How is that the key?

19. What is the real issue in Sabbath conflicts?

20. How does Sabbath breaking still bring death?

RESPONSE

1. The Pharisees intended to preserve and protect God's law. Can people who mean well do evil? Are there areas in my life where I mean well, but do wrong?

2. The Pharisees tried to protect God's law by being even stricter than God. Do I do that in my life?

3. Does my church teach that the Ten Commandments are applicable to people today? If not, has my church substituted man-made rules for God's?

4. Why did Jesus do so many miracles of healing on the Sabbath? Should I be more concerned about helping people who are sick or suffering in various ways on the Lord's Day (see James 1:27)?

5. What works of piety or worship do I do on the Lord's Day? What works of necessity? What works of mercy?

6. The Pharisees were pleased with their own behavior and quick to criticize and condemn others. Am I too easily pleased with myself and ready to point out flaws and problems in others?

7. If Jesus is Lord of the Sabbath, then what should my attitude be toward his day?

8. How can my own struggle with Sabbath-related issues ultimately be resolved?

SEVEN

KEEPING THE SABBATH HOLILY AND HAPPILY

If you call the Sabbath a delight . . .
then you will find your joy in the LORD.
—*Isaiah 58:13–14*

Welcome, delightful morn, Thou day of sacred rest!
I hail thy kind return, Lord, make these moments blest;
From the low train of mortal toys
I soar to reach immortal joys,
I soar to reach immortal joys.
—*"Hayward" in Dobell's Selections, 1806*

Sunday is supposed to be "day of all the week the best," according to the beloved author of "Amazing Grace."[1] But is that what it really is for many of us and our families?

When I was a young boy growing up in a suburb of Boston, Sunday was the longest day of the week. A remnant of Puritan Sabbath keeping lingered in the blue laws[2] regulating community activities on Sunday. Businesses were closed and so were all the stores. Unless you went to church (we usually didn't), there was nothing to do except sleep late, read the comics, and get bored.

Saturday was the best day of the week for us. Dad didn't have to work, and there were plenty of things to do and places to go (once the morning chores were done).

We only knew the Lord of the Sabbath distantly then, by reputation, the way most of us know celebrities or the president of the United States. Consequently, we didn't really have any understanding of what the Lord's Day was supposed to be and how it could bless us. We had inherited a lot of *do*s and *don't*s from our New England forefathers, but we didn't know why we were supposed to do some things and not do others on Sunday. We had the outward form of the Sabbath, but not the inward understanding that we needed to "call the Sabbath a delight" (Isaiah 58:13) and mean it.

The possession of outward form without inward understanding is called formalism, and formalism is the dry rot of today's church. A friend who installs windows once described to me what it was like to replace some windows that had been painted shut in an older cottage. It was only the paint that held the glass in place. The window frames were nothing but powder! He could push a long hat pin clear through the "wood"!

Dry rot in the church means having a form of godliness while denying its power (2 Timothy 3:5). In this spiritually stale state, people cling to certain religious traditions, like the Sabbath, and go through the motions of worship without really knowing or appreciating why they do it. Eventually they will probably stop doing even that.

McSabbath then begins to look more and more attractive to some churches as a way of preserving at least the appearance of minimal biblical order while accommodating the desires of a post-Christian (that is, neopagan) culture.

The way to preserve and protect the biblical Sabbath, however, is neither by relaxing its hold on the rhythm of life, nor by strengthening its grip by the imposition of man-made rules and regulations. The way to preserve and protect the biblical Sabbath is to keep it in the way that God intended it to be kept, with understanding of its purposes and appreciation for the blessings it brings.

We have seen that the Sabbath is a present rest, based on past events, having future reference and fulfillment in the great Day of the Lord.

In the fourth commandment, God declares that he is sovereign over time (he made it) and over our use of it (he made us!). He has from the very beginning of time appointed one day in seven as a day for rest and refreshment in him.

We all observe the Sabbath. All people everywhere do. Sunday comes along once every week without fail, and we all do something with the day. The question is not whether or not we observe the Sabbath, but how we observe it.

Some people are zealous beyond the Scriptures and bind themselves and others to rules and regulations that God never gave. The Pharisees would be proud of them.

Others are lax and fall short of the Scriptures, and of the blessings that God promises to those who will in love keep his day holy.

The central issue in Sabbath discussions today is exactly what it has always been: the authority of Jesus Christ as Lord. *How does the Lord of the Sabbath want us to use the day for our good and his glory?* That's the question we need to answer in this chapter.

"Finally," you may be thinking to yourself, "he's going to get to what I wanted in the first place. I can still have my laminated, wallet-sized list of *dos* and *don'ts*, after all."

I'm sorry, but you should know by now that life is not that simple. Refill your coffee cup if you need to, because we still have some distance to go. W. B. Trevelyan observes,

> Much of a man's real discipline consists in the effort involved in thinking out principles, and applying them to the details of daily life. It seems to be the will of Almighty God that nothing in this world of probation shall be too easy.[3]

Thinking out principles. That's the really hard part. Many of us would like to have someone in authority—a pastor, perhaps—just tell us what to do and what not to do in great detail. That would certainly make life simpler and tidier, wouldn't it? May I jog on Sunday? Go sailing in the afternoon? Mow my lawn? Go shopping at the mall? Fire up the grill for a barbecue? Chantry wisely warns,

> This sort of inquiry regarding explicit details of behaviour is, unfortunately, encouraged by a type of

church leader who feeds his ego by promoting himself as a kind of ethical guru. Wishing to be the ideal
elder or conscientious teacher this "leader" offers direction in minute particulars of living. His style of
handling practical issues of living makes his people
utterly dependent upon his counsel. His people become incapable of coping with decisions unless the
"oracle of wisdom" has decreed exact permission or
prohibition.[4]

He continues,

It was never intended that God's people be given ex-
haustively itemized delineation of what to do in
every circumstance. He did not place elders in lead-
ership so that they might dictate what specific course
to follow in every particular.

Our Lord has given us the great principles of his
Word. Also, he has sent the Holy Spirit to assist our
understanding, so that, in any given set of alterna-
tives requiring judgment, the individual saint will be
exercised in spirit. Only by inner wrestlings will he
increase in discernment of what is best.

General principles from God's Word are ade-
quate guidelines to equip a Christian, aided by the
Holy Spirit, to face every eventuality.[5]

The good news, if you are a Christian, is that you have
everything you need to figure out what God wants you to do
on the Sabbath. God has given you his Word and his Spirit.
The bad news is, you have to think, be exercised in spirit,

and experience inner wrestlings. There are no shortcuts to holiness.

What are the general principles from God's Word that will help us to keep the Sabbath as our Lord wants us to? Okay, if you really must have a laminated card and just can't live without one, you can make one that looks something like this:

- *Keep it holily.*
- *Keep it happily.*
- *Keep it honestly.*
- *Keep it humbly.*

KEEP IT HOLILY

The word *holy* refers to someone or something that is unique, distinct, set apart by God from common use for his purposes. We are called to keep or maintain the Sabbath as a day set apart by God for rest and refreshment of both body and soul.

It is important to recognize that we cannot make the Sabbath holy. God has already done that by his works of creation and redemption in the Old Testament, and by the resurrection of Jesus Christ and the gift of his Holy Spirit in the New.

The Resurrection Sabbath that we celebrate today is not identical to the Exodus Sabbath of the Old Covenant. That Sabbath, with its ceremonies and sacrifices, died with Christ and rose again on the first day of the week as the Lord's Day of the New Covenant. Thus, Paul could write to the church at Colosse,

> Therefore do not let anyone judge you by what you
> eat or drink, or with regard to a religious festival, a
> New Moon celebration or a Sabbath day. These are a
> shadow of the things that were to come; the reality,
> however, is found in Christ. (Colossians 2:16–17)

What did Paul intend by this statement? By linking "a Sabbath day" to other religious festivals that were but a shadow of the reality found in Christ, did Paul intend to do what Jesus did not, and abolish the Sabbath? Certainly not.

Clearly the Old Testament cycle was disengaged by the coming of Christ, but it is just as clear that in the New Testament the first day of the week was in fact distinguished or set apart from the other six.

The relationship between the Old Covenant and the New is not one of identity, but one of progressive continuity. This means that while the specific day and form of Sabbath observance have changed in the New Testament, the principle of Sabbath keeping remains basic to biblical faith and life. "There remains, then, a Sabbath-rest [or, Sabbath keeping[6]] for the people of God" (Hebrews 4:9).

To keep the Sabbath holy, then, means that gathering with the Lord's people on the Lord's Day for corporate worship is necessary, not optional. In the Old Testament, the sacrifices were doubled on the Sabbath. People came together at the tabernacle, the temple, and the synagogue for worship, and in their homes for fellowship. Believing men, women, and children all welcomed the Sabbath as a gift that God had given them in love, a regularly returning sign of his covenant of grace. It was a good day, a day to rest and catch your breath physically, spiritually, emotionally, and in every way.

In the New Testament, the sacrifices were not doubled: Christ is the only sufficient and efficient sacrifice for sin, offered once for all (Hebrews 7:26–27). The temple made with hands has been replaced by a spiritual house made with living stones (1 Peter 2:5). The day of the week has changed; the manner of worship has changed; but the necessity of corporate worship has not changed. The author of Hebrews pleads,

> Therefore, brothers, since we have confidence to enter the Most Holy Place by the blood of Jesus, by a new and living way opened for us through the curtain, that is, his body, and since we have a great priest over the house of God, let us draw near to God with a sincere heart in full assurance of faith, having our hearts sprinkled to cleanse us from a guilty conscience and having our bodies washed with pure water. Let us hold unswervingly to the hope we profess, for he who promised is faithful. And let us consider how we may spur one another on toward love and good deeds. Let us not give up meeting together, as some are in the habit of doing, but let us encourage one another—and all the more as you see the Day approaching. (Hebrews 10:19–25)

Notice the repetition of "let us": let us draw near to God; let us hold unswervingly to the hope that we profess; let us consider how we may spur one another on toward love and good deeds; let us not give up meeting together; let us encourage one another. And we are to do all of these things in light of the approaching Day, the Lord's great day when he will judge the peoples of the earth. A casual attitude toward participation in the services of your church is not a sign of maturity, but of spiritual degeneracy.

You and I need the Sabbath. We need all of the blessings it can communicate to us. We need the friendship and the fellowship gained by worshiping with others, and we need the stimulation and the encouragement to love, obedience, and kindness that meeting together can provide.

When Sunday is swallowed up by the weekend and loses its uniqueness, its holiness, as the Lord's Day, then you and I are the inevitable losers. We cannot, by taking shortcuts, gain what the Sabbath is designed to give us. McSabbath may scratch the immediate itch, but it cannot satisfy our souls.

Keep It Happily

The Sabbath must be a holy day, but it should also be a happy day. As Nicholas Ferrar, founder of the Little Gidding community (1625), observed, "God blessed the day and sanctified it; they must go together. If we would have it happy we must make it holy."[7]

In the presence of the great God of creation, redemption, and providence, mourning and sadness must flee away. Biblical worship is characterized not only by seriousness, but also by serious joy and celebration! Shouting, clapping, singing, and dancing were all part of the experience of our spiritual forefathers, and, if we are more subdued on the outside than they were, our hearts should rejoice no less in the presence of him whom we love. Chantry comments,

Unfortunately, few have thought very much about
the great importance of bringing joyful worship to
our God. The psalmists are an exception. For in-
stance we read in Psalm 100: "Shout for *joy* to the
LORD, all the earth. Worship the LORD with *gladness;* come before him with *joyful* songs." Although
we must confess our sins and seek grace for further sanctification, the atmosphere of worship
must not be dominated by heaviness and remorse.
Ministers must learn the enormous importance of
evoking joyful praise from the hearts of the people. A steady diet of conviction of sin alone will
make our assemblies dreary and the Lord's Day a
burden.[8]

Spiritually, the Sabbath is a symbol of salvation by grace.
It is not by my works, but by the work of God, that I can be
saved. True rest can only be found in Christ. That is surely
good reason to rejoice!

Further, the Sabbath serves as a symbol of God's righteous judgment, a witness against the unbelief and restless-
ness of proud and rebellious people. As such, it speaks to all
men without distinction and without exception. Paul proclaims,

Therefore since we are God's offspring, we should
not think that the divine being is like gold or silver
or stone—an image made by man's design and skill.
In the past God overlooked such ignorance, but now
he commands all people everywhere to repent. For
he has set a day when he will judge the world with

justice by the man he has appointed. He has given proof of this to all men by raising him from the dead. (Acts 17:29–31)

Christ's resurrection is God-given proof that he will judge the world one day, the Day of the Lord.

The centrality of the resurrection in the writings of the New Testament is apparent. What may not be quite so evident to us today is the practical importance of Christ's resurrection for our own daily joy and happiness.

Paul understood that the intangibles we seek, such as joy, happiness, and contentment, are not to be found in our physical or financial circumstances, but in the joy of knowing Christ in the power of his resurrection. He testified to the Philippians,

> I know what it is to be in need, and I know what it is to have plenty. I have learned the secret of being content in any and every situation, whether well fed or hungry, whether living in plenty or in want. I can do everything through him who gives me strength. (Philippians 4:12–13)

Where can we find such strength for living? Paul answers,

> I want to know Christ and the power of his resurrection and the fellowship of sharing in his sufferings, becoming like him in his death, and so, somehow, to attain to the resurrection from the dead. (Philippians 3:10–11)

On the Sabbath, we symbolically and really enter into the rhythm of life that God has ordained. Rested and refreshed by the power of Christ's resurrection from the dead, which we celebrate in the worship of the church, we are physically and spiritually ready to begin a new week.

Have I been beaten down by my interactions with the world? I find healing and new strength in the power of Christ on the Sabbath. Am I fearful and apprehensive about the week to come at work or at school? "I can do everything through him who gives me strength" (Philippians 4:13).

Whatever my physical, spiritual, or emotional need may be, God has given me the gift of time on the Sabbath to receive needed help through the ministry of God's Spirit, Word, and people.

REVIEW

1. What were the blue laws? Does your community treat Sunday differently than the other days of the week? If so, how?

2. What is formalism? Do you see evidence of formalism in today's church? If so, what?

3. What makes McSabbath appear more and more attractive to many churches?

4. What is the right way to preserve and protect the biblical Sabbath?

5. "The Sabbath is a _____ rest, based on _____ events, having _____ reference and fulfillment in the great Day of the Lord."

6. In what sense do all people observe the Sabbath? What, then, is the important question about Sabbath observance?

7. What two mistakes must we be careful to avoid in Sabbath observance?

8. What is the central issue in Sabbath conflicts today?

9. What is the "really hard part" of Sabbath observance? Why is it so hard?

10. What would many people rather do? Why is that not a good idea?

11. According to Chantry, what two gifts has God given us to equip us to answer our questions about Sabbath keeping?

12. What are the general principles from God's Word that will help us to keep the Sabbath as our Lord wants us to?

13. What does the word *holy* mean? In what sense is the Sabbath a holy day?

14. Does the fourth commandment require New Covenant believers to keep the Sabbath in the same way as believers who lived under the Old Covenant? Why or why not?

15. What is the role of corporate worship in keeping the Sabbath day holy?

16. "Biblical worship is characterized not only by _____, but also by serious _____ and _____!"

17. How is the Sabbath a symbol of salvation by grace?

18. How is the Sabbath a symbol of God's righteous judgment?

19. How should the historical event of Christ's resurrection, which took place so many years ago, affect my daily joy and happiness today?

20. What does the Sabbath specifically and uniquely contribute toward meeting my weekly spiritual needs?

RESPONSE

1. Is Sunday "day of all the week the best" for me and my family? Why or why not?

2. Sunday blue laws used to dominate community life in Puritan New England. In principle, should the civil government support Sabbath keeping? Why or why not? What Scripture passages might apply?

3. Is it possible to really keep the Sabbath without knowing (and loving) the Lord of the Sabbath? Why or why not?

4. How is formalism in the church like dry rot? Is there any evidence of formalism in your church life? What will you do about it, if there is?

5. In review question #7 above, you identified two common mistakes we must seek to avoid in keeping the Sabbath day holy. Do you see tendencies toward either of those errors in your own life? In your church? How can you avoid them?

6. What is so hard about thinking out principles? What are we afraid of? How can we minimize that fear?

7. How can I keep the Sabbath day holy? How can I keep works of necessity to a minimum? What special activities of rest, worship, and mercy can I do that will keep this day different from the other six?

8. What is the level of my participation in the corporate worship of my church? Allowing for such factors as age

and health, am I as regular in attendance as I should be? What is the harm to me if I am not? What is the harm to the church body?

9. What can I do to encourage greater joy in the corporate worship of my church family?

10. Does the Sabbath have an evangelistic application? If so, how can I make effective use of it?

11. If the resurrection of Jesus from the dead is central to the message of the New Testament, how central should it be in my life? Is it? If it is not, what can I do about that?

12. Do I really need the Sabbath? Why?

EIGHT

KEEPING THE SABBATH
HONESTLY AND HUMBLY

Honor it by not going your own way
and not doing as you please or speaking idle words.
—*Isaiah 58:13*

Now may the King descend, And fill his throne of grace;
Thy scepter, Lord, extend, While saints address thy face;
Let sinners feel thy quick'ning Word,
And learn to know and fear the Lord,
And learn to know and fear the Lord.
Descend, celestial Dove, With all thy quick'ning pow'rs;
Disclose a Saviour's love, And bless these sacred hours;
Then shall my soul new life obtain,
Nor Sabbaths e'er be spent in vain,
Nor Sabbaths e'er be spent in vain.
—*"Hayward" in Dobell's Selections, 1806*

Ben Patterson, a contributing editor to *Christianity Today,* calls attention to the conflicting feelings that many Christians have toward the Sabbath:

> They know it is special, and to be observed, but they don't really know why or how. . . . So they always seem to be looking for loopholes: ways to get credit for keeping the Sabbath, without actually having to keep the Sabbath.[1]

We have seen so far that we must keep the Sabbath holy. It is not a day for common or ordinary use, but an extraordinary time set apart by the Lord and Creator of time to be a blessing and refreshment to his people.

We also understand that we must keep the Sabbath happily. For people who love the God of all grace, having the privilege of spending a whole day with the Father, Son, and Holy Spirit with no other obligations put upon us is no reason for gloom and doom, but for great joy and gladness.

In this chapter, we want to look at two more broad principles and how they can help us know how to keep the Sabbath as God wants us to.

KEEP IT HONESTLY

The Sabbath is a day for engaging in corporate worship and activities of personal piety, but not exclusively. Physical, emotional, and even intellectual rest is part of the "rest" that the Scriptures require of us when we cease from our six days of work.

God is concerned with our bodies as well as our souls. And why not? He made us whole beings, not bodiless spirits!

I don't think I need to define for you what work is. You don't need 1,500 rules to keep. We all have a way of recognizing work when it comes our way.

Be honest with yourself and with God. We speak of our jobs (carpenter, mechanic, salesman, secretary, executive) as our work. We also label certain activities as work: housework, yard work, and homework.

On the Sabbath, we need to cease from our works and rest in God's. As Patterson wryly notes, "Seven days of work make one weak."[2]

However, not all activity is work. Rest does not require idleness. Rest can also be active. Throughout the Old Testament, rest is defined as refreshment. The word used in Scripture is related to "breath." To rest or to be refreshed is to catch our breath or to receive new breath.

This word is also related to God's act of creation, when he *breathed* into the helpless form that he had made from the dust of the ground and man received life (Genesis 2:7). Our word *recreation* is similarly related. To *recreate* is to restore, refresh, or put fresh life into someone or something. Recreation is any lawful activity that renews the body or soul.

Recreation, therefore, is a necessary part of life. The Puritans have sometimes been represented as being against recreation. That's not really accurate. The Puritans were not against relaxing, playing, and enjoying various forms of recreation. The challenge for them was how to do these and all things for the glory of God (1 Corinthians 10:31). Puritan John Winthrop (1588–1649), the first governor of the Massachusetts Bay Colony, explains:

When I had some tyme abstained from suche worldly
delights as my heart most desired, I grewe very
melancholick and uncomfortable, for I had been
more careful to refraine from an outward conversation in the world, then to keepe the love of the world
out of my heart, or to uphold my conversation in
heaven; which caused that my comfort in God
failinge, and I not daringe to meddle with any
earthly delights, I grewe into a great dullnesse and
discontent: which beinge at last perceived, I examined my heart, and findinge it needfull to recreate
my minde with some outward recreation, I yielded
unto it, and by a moderate exercise herein was much
refreshed; but here grewe the mischiefe: I per-
ceivinge that God and mine own conscience did
alowe me so to doe in my need, I afterwards tooke
occasion, from the benefite of Christian libertie, to
pretend need of recreation when there was none,
and so by degrees I ensnared my heart so farre in
worldly delights, as I cooled the graces of the spirit
by them: Whereby I perceive that in all outward com-
forts, althoughe God allows us the use of the things
themselves, yet it must be in sobriety, and our hearts
must be kept free, for he is jealous of our love, and
will not endure any pretences in it.[3]

Trying to keep the love of the world out of his heart,
Winthrop first abstained from recreational activities. The
spiritual result was not what he expected. He grew dull and
discontented, found his comfort in God failing, and became
spiritually depressed ("melancholick"). Recognizing that

something was wrong, Winthrop examined his heart and realized that his mind needed to be refreshed by some form of outward recreation. He introduced some moderate exercise and felt himself renewed, both physically and spiritually. God and his conscience seemed to agree that some recreation could be allowed. However, little by little ("by degrees") Winthrop found his pursuit of recreation interfering with his fellowship with God. He pretended to need recreation when he did not, and the graces of the Spirit in his life cooled as he pursued worldly delights. Excessive indulgence in things that might otherwise be lawful in themselves can become a form of idolatry.

Is any kind of recreation appropriate on the Sabbath? The Puritans recognized that recreational activities had some value in general, but they did not see how recreation could in any way serve the purposes of the Sabbath. Their exclusion of recreation was based, at least in part, on what Beckwith and Stott term "a doubtful interpretation" of Isaiah 58:13–14.[4] The text says,

> "If you keep your feet from breaking the Sabbath and from doing as you please on my holy day, if you call the Sabbath a delight and the LORD's holy day honorable, and if you honor it by not going your own way and not doing as you please or speaking idle words, then you will find your joy in the LORD, and I will cause you to ride on the heights of the land and to feast on the inheritance of your father Jacob." The mouth of the LORD has spoken.

While some commentators believe that going your own way, doing as you please, and speaking idle words all have to do with the pursuit of business, others believe the prohibition applies to almost anything that brings personal pleasure.

Pink echoed the Puritans[5] by forbidding "natural recreations and doing our own pleasure"[6] on the Sabbath. Similarly, Pipa argues, " 'Doing your pleasure' refers to those things you enjoy doing or must do the other six days: business, work, play, or whatever. When you do these things on God's holy day you desecrate it."[7]

To some degree, both of these positions seem to miss the point. Sabbath keeping should neither be limited to avoiding business transactions on Sunday nor expanded to prohibiting everything you enjoy.

Isaiah brings the central issue of the Sabbath controversy into clear and bold focus. Whose day is it? Who is the Lord of the Sabbath, and will I bow before him? How does the Lord of the Sabbath want me to use the day for my good and his glory?

As Beckwith and Stott note, the expression "doing as you please" "may well refer to wilfulness rather than to recreation."[8] The point of the passage is not so much that we must avoid doing anything fun or pleasurable on the Sabbath as that we must "take captive every thought to make it obedient to Christ" (2 Corinthians 10:5).

In love, we must labor to bring our wills into submission to his. The Sabbath calls us to make God's will our own, so that when we do what he tells us to do we are in fact doing what we want to do.

What about recreation? To the degree that recreation contributes to our physical and spiritual renewal, some moderate recreation may be admissible on the Sabbath. Chantry takes a biblical and reasonable approach to such particular questions.

> More rests upon motive and intent than upon the outward acts we do on the Sabbath. "May I go bicycle-riding on Sunday?" Because younger children are not equipped to discern their own heart motives or the application of general principles, parents must make some rules for their households. Perhaps one family will have children who are so attached to bicycle-riding on six days of the week, that they will tell their children, "No bicycle-riding on Sunday." They intend to make the day special by filling it with different activity on the Lord's Day.
>
> As soon as one parent tells his child, "We do not ride bicycles on Sunday; it is the Lord's Day," along will come a Christian neighbour with his children— all riding bicycles! His motive may have been to give his young children necessary exercise so that they can be still at evening worship.[9]

What kind of recreation may be appropriate? As we "think out principles," we will not always agree on how to apply them. We must be prepared to think the best of those who may in good conscience reach different conclusions than we do. John Calvin was refreshed by lawn bowling on Sunday afternoons. Should we think less of him if our consciences hesitate to do as he did? Chantry warns,

> Legalistic and Pharisaic minds will imagine that if they cannot jog and still keep the Sabbath holy, then neither

can any of their brothers. This is just the way man-made rules begin to be made and oppressive traditions start.[10]

It may be helpful to ask yourself these or similar questions concerning any proposed activity:

- Will it in fact refresh me, or will I be worn out?
- Is a competitive spirit, as in league sports, compatible with the purpose of refreshment and of the Sabbath? What if I lose?
- Will a planned recreational activity interfere with my previous commitment to corporate worship and fellowship? If I do this, will it cause me to miss or be late to the evening service of my church?
- Is my will subordinated to the will of God, or am I "doing my own thing" and thus doing as I please on God's holy day? Is what pleases me what pleases God?
- Can I do what I am thinking of doing to the glory of God?

Take Governor Winthrop's example and warning to heart. Be careful you don't by degrees turn liberty into license and make God's holy day your play day. But, at the same time, don't be so afraid to experience pleasure that you turn dancing into mourning. The Sabbath really is a day for rejoicing and relaxing with both your natural and spiritual families.

KEEP IT HUMBLY

The Sabbath is admittedly a problem for many Christians.

I am convinced that the problem is not intellectual. The biblical data are sufficient to show that the Sabbath has something to do with us. Even those brothers and sisters who do not believe in the perpetuity of the moral law—that the Ten Commandments (including the fourth) are the standard for Christian living—treat Sunday differently than they do the other days of the week.

Nor is the problem a practical one. Sure, there may be questions and even disagreements about particular activities, but those questions are really very small when we understand what the basic principles and purposes of the Lord's Day are.

No, the problem that many Christians have with the Sabbath is primarily spiritual in nature. Sometimes people ask why Sabbath keeping is such a big deal. It seems like such a small matter to us. But why does it seem like such a small matter to us? Because of the rebellion in our hearts. We are the heirs of centuries of self-exaltation, and our minds are not yet submitted to the Word of God. On the inside, we still resist God's right to rule over us.

Even Christian people commonly hold the day in light esteem, as nothing more than a second Saturday to catch up on all the housework, yard work, homework, and office work that we didn't get done on the other six days of the week.

Sunday has lost its special place in our busy world. As reporter Maureen Hayden observes,

> For millions of Americans, Sundays may be just like any other day of the week.
>
> Gone are the "blue laws" that kept merchant's doors closed and elevated church as the main reason to get dressed up and venture out of the house.
>
> But it's not just shopping that fills our Sundays.

Everything from work to weekend chores to the kids' ball games may be consuming the hours once devoted to rest, worship and family.[11]

We come into our King's presence and our spiritual family reunion tired, late, and unprepared to worship him—if we make it at all. This is not right. If we were this careless in our worldly occupations, we would soon be unemployed. If we treated our natural families and friends with such disrespect, we would soon lose them.

On almost any Sunday afternoon, you will find thousands of people crammed into some sports arena or stadium to cheer on their home team. They prepared for this event. They checked the team schedule and wrote this date on their calendar. They set aside some of their paycheck and bought the best tickets they thought they could afford. They will go to bed at a decent hour so that on the big day they will be rested and able to enjoy the game. They will plan to drive in early so that they can find good parking and not be late. Once in the stadium, they will sit for hours on uncomfortable seats or benches without complaining. They are not ashamed to be called fans (short for *fanatics*). They will shout and cheer and clap their hands and have a wonderful time.

But next Sunday morning, look around you. Where are the crowds to clap and cheer and praise the Lord? They're all at home, sleeping in. It was too hard to get out of bed this morning. They're too tired after being out partying until two in the morning. Or they're heading for the ski slopes. Or the lake. Or the office. There's too much to do and too little time during the week, so they steal the time that God has specifically set apart for enjoying him and celebrating his works.

Thinking themselves wise, they are actually robbing their own souls. Patterson laments, "What do we lose when we lose the Sabbath? We lose grace."[12] Like the greedy merchants that Amos confronted (Amos 8:4–7), people want the Sabbath to be over so they can get back to business as usual. And just like those merchants, and like the people of Israel and the church of today, they are restless and dissatisfied. They wonder why they do not grow spiritually. Why does God seem so distant, and the church so weak? Could it be that grace is leaking out of our earthen vessels like water through a sieve?

Sabbath keeping is a means of grace to all who love the Lord. Hear what our God says through his prophet:

> To the eunuchs who keep my Sabbaths, who choose what pleases me and hold fast to my covenant—to them I will give within my temple and its walls a memorial and a name better than sons and daughters; I will give them an everlasting name that will not be cut off. And foreigners who bind themselves to the LORD to serve him, to love the name of the LORD, and to worship him, all who keep the Sabbath without desecrating it and who hold fast to my covenant—these I will bring to my holy mountain and give them joy in my house of prayer. Their burnt offerings and sacrifices will be accepted on my altar; for my house will be called a house of prayer for all nations. (Isaiah 56:4–7)

The way to gain a name and a blessing is not by building it yourself, but by humbly choosing what pleases God, resting in his works, and keeping his covenant and his Sabbath holy. Sabbath wars must all come to an end in Christ, the Prince of Peace.

> All praise to God the Father be,
> All praise, eternal Son, to thee,
> Whom with the Spirit, we adore
> Forever and forever more.
>
> (William Walsham How, 1871)

REVIEW

1. What are the conflicting feelings that many Christians have toward Sabbath keeping?
2. Should I spend the whole Sabbath only in corporate and personal worship? Why or why not?
3. What is the relationship between rest, refreshment, and breath?
4. What is recreation? Is it a necessary part of life?
5. What can happen to us, physically and spiritually, if we don't get any exercise?
6. Can things that are lawful in themselves become wrong? If so, under what circumstances? What did Governor Winthrop discover about his pursuit of recreation?
7. Can any kind of recreation be appropriate to the Sabbath? Why or why not?
8. Does Isaiah 58:13–14 forbid all recreation on the Sabbath? What is the point of the passage?
9. Chantry notes, "More rests upon _____ and _____ than upon the outward acts we do on the Sabbath." Do you agree or disagree? Why?

10. Will Christians who are honestly trying to make their thoughts captive to Christ always agree on every application of Scripture? How should we handle our disagreements?

11. Does Christian liberty mean that Christ gives others liberty to do some things that I may not allow myself to do?

12. What are some helpful questions to ask about any proposed activity on the Sabbath?

13. Is the Sabbath "problem" primarily an intellectual one for most Christians? What kind of problem is it?

14. Why does Sabbath keeping seem to be a minor issue to many people?

15. According to Patterson, what do we lose when we lose the Sabbath?

16. What is the only real resolution possible for the Sabbath wars?

Response

1. Do I share in the conflicting feelings that many seem to have toward the Sabbath? How? What is my attitude?

2. Do I, or does my church, minimize the importance of physical, emotional, and mental rest on the Sabbath?

3. Is my Sabbath so full of organized activities that I have no time for physical rest and relaxation or spiritual reflection?

4. Do I cheat when I try to define work? How? Why?

5. When the Sabbath is over, do I more often feel refreshed or exhausted? Why? Should I be doing something differently than I am to keep the Sabbath holy?

6. What kinds of physical activities relax and refresh me? Are any of them things that I can do on the Lord's Day?

7. In consideration of Isaiah 58:13–14, does what pleases me on the Sabbath agree with what pleases God, or do I still disagree with him?

8. What is my attitude toward those whose conclusions concerning acceptable Sabbath activities differ from my own? What should my attitude be? Do I need an attitude adjustment?

9. Do I use Sunday as a "second Saturday?" Is that keeping the Sabbath holy?

10. Am I as concerned to prepare for the Sabbath as sports fans are to go to "the big game"? If not, why not? What changes do I need to make in the patterns of my life to be ready to enjoy God and celebrate his works of creation and redemption with the rest of my spiritual family?

11. Do I long for the Sabbath to be over so I can get back to business as usual? What does that reveal about my heart?

12. What is the only way the Sabbath war in my heart can be resolved? Have I made peace with the Lord of the Sabbath?

NOTES

Chapter 1: McSabbath

1   "Israeli Franchisee Fights to Stay Open on Sabbath," *Seattle Times,* March 23, 1997.

2   Erik Lacitis, "Holy Moses! Updated 'Shalls' for the '90s," *Seattle Times,* February 2, 1997.

3   These conflicts, which may be internal or external, are part of a much larger confrontation. Psalm 2:1–3 says, "Why do the nations conspire and the peoples plot in vain? The kings of the earth take their stand and the rulers gather together against the LORD and against his Anointed One. 'Let us break their chains,' they say, 'and throw off their fetters.' "

4   Second Corinthians 5:9 says, "So we make it our goal to please him, whether we are at home in the body or away from it."

5   W. J. Chantry, *Call the Sabbath a Delight* (Edinburgh: Banner of Truth, 1991), 20.

Chapter 2: The Fourth Commandment

1   John Newton, *The Works of John Newton* (Edinburgh: Banner of Truth, 1985), 3:504.

2   J. H. Primus, "Calvin and the Puritan Sabbath: a Comparative Study," in *Exploring the Heritage of John Calvin,* ed. D. E. Holwerda (Grand Rapids: Baker, 1976), 40.

3   The book that I have found most helpful in approaching the Sabbath issue has been R. T. Beckwith and W. Stott, *This Is the Day* (London: Marshall, Morgan, and Scott, 1978), published in the U.S. under the title *The Christian Sunday* (Grand Rapids: Baker, 1978).

4   Dorothy C. Bass, "Rediscovering the Sabbath," *Christianity Today* 41, no. 10 (September 1, 1997): 39–40.

5   Ibid., 40.

6   Augustine, *Confessions* 11.14, as cited in Niels-Erik Andreasen, *The Christian Use of Time* (Nashville: Abingdon, 1978), 12.

7   For more on this, see Paul K. Jewett, *The Lord's Day* (Grand Rapids: Eerdmans, 1971), 15–16.

CHAPTER 3: SABBATH OR LORD'S DAY? OLD TESTAMENT ROOTS

1   J. Douma, *The Ten Commandments* (Phillipsburg, N.J.: P&R, 1996), 144.

2   Cited in ibid., 146.

3   R. J. Rushdoony, *The Institutes of Biblical Law* (Nutley, N.J.: Craig Press, 1973), 154.

4   See G. Vos, *Biblical Theology* (Grand Rapids: Eerdmans, 1948), 14–17.

5   Augustine: ". . . the Old Testament revealed in the New, the New veiled in the Old" (quoted in P. Schaff, ed., *The Nicene and Post-Nicene Fathers* [Grand Rapids: Eerdmans, 1956], 8:531).

6   F. N. Lee, *The Covenantal Sabbath* (London: Lord's Day Observance Society, 1969), 67.

7   See J. Murray, *Principles of Conduct* (Grand Rapids: Eerdmans, 1957), 27–44.

8   Ibid., 32.

9   Ibid., 34. Murray goes on to argue that Genesis 2:2–3 is sufficient to establish that the Sabbath "must have been known by Adam and his contemporaries."

10 Lee, *The Covenantal Sabbath,* 51–134. Lee is always interesting, if not always convincing.

11 Ibid., 146.

12 H. Gressmann, *Altorientalische Texte zum alten Testament,* 329, cited by E. Lohse in *Theological Dictionary of the New Testament,* vol. 7, ed. Gerhard Friedrich, trans. Geoffrey W. Bromiley (Grand Rapids: Eerdmans, 1971), 2.

13 This is one reason, by the way, why we should not give up the evening service in our evangelical and Reformed churches.

14   J. Telushkin, *Jewish Literacy* (New York: William Morrow and Company, 1991), 148–58.

15   See chapter 6.

Chapter 4: Sabbath or Lord's Day? New Testament Flower and Fruits

1   Some want to deny that circumcision and baptism are related, but see Colossians 2:11–13. Both outward signs (circumcision and baptism) point to the same inward spiritual reality of regeneration. Physical circumcision in the Old Testament declares the necessity of removing the defilement of sin and the necessity of new birth, anticipating the spiritual circumcision of the hearts of God's elect by the Holy Spirit. In a similar way, but from a different perspective, water baptism in the New Testament celebrates the reality of the inward new birth accomplished by the power of God's Spirit. Thus, the relationship between the two ordinances, like the relationship between the two covenants, is one of anticipation and accomplishment. Circumcision looks forward to the work of God's Spirit and says, "You must be born again." Baptism looks back to the accomplishment of that work of grace and testifies, "I have been born again."

2   There is no one text that explicitly says this. The reader should consider the evidence that follows and judge whether or not it agrees with Scripture.

3   "Whatever may have changed in the transition from the Sabbath to Sunday, the fourth commandment continues, along with the other nine commandments, to be valid for the church today *as a commandment.*" J. Douma, *The Ten Commandments* (Phillipsburg, N.J.: P&R, 1996), 130.

4   The NIV translates this word as "comfort."

5   Exodus 23:16; 34:22; Leviticus 23:15–21; Numbers 28:26–31; Deuteronomy 16:9–12. Pentecost was the second of the three major annual festivals at which every male Israelite was required to appear before the Lord at his sanctuary (Deuteronomy 16:16).

6   These were known languages. Acts 2:8–11 say, "Then how is it that each of us hears them in his own native language? Parthians, Medes

and Elamites; residents of Mesopotamia, Judea and Cappadocia, Pontus and Asia, Phrygia and Pamphylia, Egypt and the parts of Libya near Cyrene; visitors from Rome (both Jews and converts to Judaism); Cretans and Arabs—we hear them declaring the wonders of God in our own tongues!"

7   F. N. Lee, *The Covenantal Sabbath* (London: Lord's Day Observance Society, 1969), 30 n. 206: "According to the fourth gospel (cf. John 18:28; 19:14), Good Friday was the 14th Nisan; in which case the day of Unleavened Bread of that year was the 16th Nisan on a Sunday, whence the following Feast of Pentecost must correspondingly also have fallen on a Sunday."

8   Christopher Wordsworth, 1862.

9   Some people object to calling the Lord's Day "the Sabbath." But "to argue that the Lord's Day cannot be called the Christian Sabbath when, as a matter of fact, it is related to the Sabbath as it is, would be the more doubtful position to espouse." P. K. Jewett, *The Lord's Day* (Grand Rapids: Eerdmans, 1971), 122.

10   "It may well be that all of Christ's important manifestations between Resurrection or Easter Sunday and Pentecost Sunday took place on successive Sundays." Lee, *The Covenantal Sabbath,* 207.

11   R. T. Beckwith and W. Stott, *The Christian Sunday* (Grand Rapids: Baker, 1978), 30.

12   First Corinthians 11:26 says, "For whenever you eat this bread and drink this cup, you proclaim the Lord's death until he comes." See also Matthew 26:29; Mark 14:25; Luke 22:16, 18.

13   To set the context, read Hebrews 3:7–4:11.

14   W. J. Chantry, *Call the Sabbath a Delight* (Edinburgh: Banner of Truth, 1991), 90.

15   Ibid., 90–91.

16   Douma, *The Ten Commandments,* 141.

17   *Sabbatismos* in Greek.

18   See Exodus 16:30; Leviticus 23:32; 26:34–35; 2 Chronicles 36:21.

19   Cited in J. A. Pipa, *The Lord's Day* (Fearn, Scotland: Christian Focus, 1997), 116 n. 6.

20   Ibid., 117.

21   A. W. Pink, *An Exposition of Hebrews,* 2 vols. (Grand Rapids: Baker, 1967), 210. Cited in Pipa, *The Lord's Day,* 118.

22   Pipa, *The Lord's Day,* 117–18.

CHAPTER 5: SABBATH WARS: THE CONFLICT BEGUN

1   A. W. Pink, *The Ten Commandments* (Swengel, Pa.: Reiner Publications, 1971), 29.

2   M. J. Dawn, *Keeping the Sabbath Wholly* (Grand Rapids: Eerdmans, 1989), 29.

3   Ibid., 57.

4   H. W. F. Saggs, *The Might That Was Assyria* (London: Sidgwick & Jackson, 1984), 268.

5   S. Moscati, *Ancient Semitic Civilizations* (New York: G. P. Putnam's Sons, 1960), 59.

6   The proposition that if anything can go wrong, it will go wrong, formulated by American engineer E. A. Murphy, Jr., in 1949.

7   B. Maoz, "Israel under Crossfire," in the Christian Witness to Israel *Herald* (spring 1996): 5.

8   Thus, legalism produces the opposite effects of free and sovereign grace. See Psalm 30:10–12.

CHAPTER 6: SABBATH WARS: THE BATTLE WON

1   J. Calvin, *Commentary on a Harmony of the Evangelists, Matthew, Mark, and Luke,* trans. William Pringle (1563; Edinburgh: Calvin Translation Society, 1845; reprinted in *Calvin's Commentaries,* vol. 16, by Baker, 1979), 1:281–82.

2   J. C. Ryle, *Knots Untied* (London: James Clarke & Co., 1964), 239.

3   R. Cecil in J. H. Pratt, ed., *The Thought of the Evangelical Leaders* (Edinburgh: Banner of Truth, 1978), 42.

4   The word "fulfill" simply means to "fill full." Some creative commentators stretch it to mean "abrogate" or "abolish," thus making Jesus say, "Do not think that I have come to abolish the Law or the Prophets; I have not come to abolish them but to *abolish* them"!

5   See also the parallel passages Matthew 12:1–8 and Luke 6:1–5.

6   G. I. Williamson, *The Westminster Confession of Faith for Study Classes* (Philadelphia: Presbyterian & Reformed, 1964), 171.

7   See the parallel passages Matthew 12:9–14 and Luke 6:6–11.

8   Contrary to popular evangelical sensitivity, there are times when anger is the only proper response of a righteous person. The counsel of Ephesians 4:26 is not to avoid anger altogether, but to avoid *sinning* in your anger. J. C. Ryle warns, "A sinless wrath is a very rare thing" (*Expository Thoughts on St. Mark* [London: Hodder and Stoughton, 1896], 48).

9   The Herodians made it their business to please the Roman authorities. Sin really does make strange bedfellows!

10   This verb ("throw out") may mean that he was excommunicated from the synagogue.

11   Westminster Confession of Faith, 21.8.

12   J. C. Ryle, *Expository Thoughts on St. Mark,* 42–43.

13   There are differences between the nationalistic Old Covenant theocracy and the supranational New Covenant church in the administration of Sabbath observance by civil authorities. "The Master reminds us of God's judgment but stipulates no civil reprisals for breaking the Sabbath." See W. J. Chantry, *Call the Sabbath a Delight* (Edinburgh: Banner of Truth, 1991), 61–70.

14   R. M. M'Cheyne, "I Love the Lord's Day," in A. A. Bonar, *Robert Murray M'Cheyne: Memoir and Remains* (London: Banner of Truth, 1966), 597.

CHAPTER 7: KEEPING THE SABBATH HOLILY AND HAPPILY

1   John Newton, *The Works of John Newton* (Edinburgh: Banner of Truth, 1985), 3:504.

2   They were so named because they were originally printed on blue paper.

3   W. B. Trevelyan, *Sunday* (London: Longmans, Green, and Co., 1903), 3.

4   W. J. Chantry, *Call the Sabbath a Delight* (Edinburgh: Banner of Truth, 1991), 104.

5   Ibid., 105.

6   So S. M. Baugh, cited in J. A. Pipa, *The Lord's Day* (Fearn, Scotland: Christian Focus, 1997), 116 n. 6.

7   N. Ferrar, cited in A. L. Maycock, *Nicholas Ferrar of Little Gidding* (Grand Rapids: Eerdmans, 1980), 208.

8   Chantry, *Call the Sabbath a Delight,* 37.

CHAPTER 8: KEEPING THE SABBATH HONESTLY AND HUMBLY

1   B. Patterson, "Rest? Never on Sunday," *Christianity Today* 30, no. 13 (September 19, 1986): 16–17.

2   Ibid., 16.

3   J. Winthrop, *Winthrop Papers* (Boston: Massachusetts Historical Society, 1929), 1:201–2. Cited in E. S. Morgan, *The Puritan Family* (New York: Harper & Row, 1966), 17.

4   R. T. Beckwith and W. Stott, *The Christian Sunday* (Grand Rapids: Baker, 1978), 145 n. 18.

5   See the Westminster Confession of Faith, 21.8.

6   A. W. Pink, *The Ten Commandments* (Swengel, Pa.: Reiner Publications, 1971), 31.

7   J. A. Pipa, *The Lord's Day* (Fearn, Scotland: Christian Focus, 1997), 18.

8   Beckwith and Stott, *The Christian Sunday,* 145 n. 18.

9   W. J. Chantry, *Call the Sabbath a Delight* (Edinburgh: Banner of Truth, 1991), 106.

10   Ibid., 107.

11   M. Hayden, "Sunday Loses Its Special Place in a Busy World," *The Eastside Journal,* August 15, 1998.

12   Patterson, "Rest? Never on Sunday," 16.